A HANDBOOK TO THE PALACE OF MINOS AT KNOSSOS

GENERAL EDITOR

WILFRID J. MILLINGTON SYNGE

Arthur J. Evans

A HANDBOOK TO THE

PALACE OF MINOS KNOSSOS

WITH ITS DEPENDENCIES

J. D. S. PENDLEBURY

CURATOR MCMXXIX-XXXIV

FOREWORD

SIR ARTHUR EVANS

INTRODUCTION

SIR JOHN MYRES

SIR JOHN FORSDYKE

MACDONALD : LONDON

First published in this edition in 1954 by
MAX PARRISH AND CO LTD

Sixth Impression, 1969

Published by
Macdonald & Co. (Publishers) Ltd.,
St. Giles House, 49 Poland Street,
London, W.1.

Made and printed in Great Britain by
A. Wheaton & Co., Exeter

CONTENTS

ILLUSTRATIONS

PLANS

FOREWORD

In fulfilment of my own desires, Mr. Pendlebury has excellently carried out the plan of a summary guide to the House of Minos and its immediate surroundings. In the works of reconstitution, which here so necessarily followed that of the spade, the object of affording an intelligible picture to the visitor had been constantly kept in view. The replacement where possible in situ *of the frescoes fallen from the walls by Monsieur Gilliéron's admirable restorations has supplied some samples at least of the original brilliant decoration.*

It is true that the existing remains of the building, once with tiers of upper stories on all sides, leave vast lacunas. The name 'Labyrinth' indeed, which itself stands for the 'House of the labrys*' or sacred double axe of old Cretan and Anatolian cult, has led to much popular misconception. But the idea of a maze – to which the complex impression given by parts of the basements might seem to lend some support – was far from the conception of its builders. The Palace itself, and notably the* piano nobile *of the West Quarter, was a crescendo of spacious corridors, peristyles, and halls served beyond by a stately staircase. The 'Grand Staircase' again of the East Quarter, where the main approach was from above, was of a unique quality amongst ancient buildings. On the other hand, the arrangement of the reception rooms in the more public suites of state usage and the more private section where we may place the quarters of the women and children is a masterpiece of architectural planning.*

It is now some forty years since – lured by the visions of the earliest folk traditions of Greece and encouraged by such indications as were to be extracted from seal-stones and the signs of an unknown script – I first explored the site, at a time when, though minor relics of great promise abounded, there was nothing visible above ground beyond the tumbled remains of a wall above the southern slope.

The work of the spade has now brought out the essential underlying truth of the old traditions that made Knossos – the home of

Minos and Daedalos – the most ancient centre of civilized life in Greece and with it, of our whole Continent. It may be confidently said indeed, that no equal plot of Earth's surface has been productive in such various directions of so many unique records bearing on our earliest culture. Not only have we here the first evidences of an advanced linear script, but architecture is already fully developed on novel lines, and with a no less original form of fresco decoration carried to great perfection, while masterpieces in sculpture and moulding have here come to light – from the ivory figure of the leaping youth to the forepart of the charging bull in painted stucco from the Northern Portico and the high reliefs of parts of athletic human figures from the Great East Hall – which for instantaneous spirit and truth to natural forms have in their own line never been surpassed.

The originals of these must be visited in the Museum at Candia. Though of old a Palace, the 'Labyrinth' of which in spite of clearing and partial reconstitution we have only today a fragment of a fragment, is discontinuous in many directions and in places artificially linked. The visitor who wishes to explore its full circuit still needs the guidance that of old was provided by Ariadne's clew.

ARTHUR EVANS

PREFACE

It has been evident for some time that there ought to be a short guide to Knossos. Not only is the owner of a 1909 *Baedeker* liable to be entirely at sea and to wander in a state of complete bewilderment round a labyrinth in many respects unrecognizable, but the fortunate possessors of *The Palace of Minos* have hesitated before hiring the pack animal necessary for the transport of that monumental work round the site.

Of course there is only one man who could have written this guide as it ought to have been written – Sir Arthur Evans – but in view of the Herculean labours in which he is engaged, I hope that visitors will excuse my temerity in making the attempt. How great my debt has been both to Sir Arthur and to Dr. Mackenzie only I can say. Without their guidance I should have been as completely lost as Theseus without the clew of Ariadne.

The plan of the guide is as follows. I have first given an introductory Section on the history of the site, mainly from the point of view of the architectural development of the Palace. This, I think, was inevitable. Nobody wants either to be unexpectedly faced with a totally meaningless combination of letters such as 'Late M.M. III*b*' or to be held up while going round the site by having to read a lot of information, mostly quite irrelevant to his present position, about the general layout of the Palace at a particular period. I have therefore set this section first.

Then comes the grand tour of the Palace proper, by what experience has proved to be the best route. Lastly the outlying buildings are described.

Plan No. 9 has the route adopted marked with arrows, and there are a few photographs to assist in the identification of landmarks.

I must apologize for addressing the visitor throughout in the second person. There are two other methods, first the impersonal 'one', which always seems so lonely, secondly the use of 'we', which is undoubtedly the cause of so many single visitors looking uneasily over their shoulders for some unseen companion.

The excavation of the Palace of Minos at Knossos is one of the most important historical events of the century. Schliemann, with his extraordinary flair, had intended to dig here, but at that time the political and other difficulties to be faced were insuperable. Sir Arthur Evans had spent some years travelling in the island, collecting seal-stones and evidences of the prehistoric script which they betrayed. In 1894 he had gained a foothold on the site, and when conditions became easier, on the arrival of Prince George, in 1900 he began the systematic excavation of Knossos. At first a Cretan Exploration Fund was formed, but for many years now Sir Arthur has borne the expense as well as the glory of the work.

Thanks to his labours and those of his assistant, Dr. Duncan Mackenzie, the prehistoric civilization of Crete has been revealed. His fellow workers in the field of Minoan archaeology have made discoveries of the utmost importance for the illumination of particular periods and sites; but nowhere, save at Knossos, is the whole evidence to hand, and if Knossos was the only site excavated we should still have a clear historical outline.

The difficulties of excavation have been many. Succeeding periods have left succeeding floor levels which must be disentangled, and the mere technical problems, such as the clearing of the Grand Staircase, were enormous.

With a building such as this, rising many stories in height, it has always been a question of how to preserve the evidence of upper floors. This has been solved by roofing in various parts of the palace and by raising to their proper level the door-jambs, column-bases, and paving-blocks which had fallen into the rooms below.

Without restoration the Palace would be a meaningless heap of ruins, the more so because the gypsum stone, of which most of the paving slabs as well as the column-bases and door-jambs are made, melts like sugar under the action of rain, and would eventually disappear completely. The accuracy of the restorations has been ensured by careful study of the evidence during the course of excavation. The yellow brown concrete beams follow the same 'chases' as their charred wooden originals. The shape and decoration of the columns, the architraves and cornices have been taken from frescoes as well as from actual evidence found on the spot.

In conclusion I may give the following chronological table which embodies the results of thirty years' work and is now generally accepted. It is based mainly on the changes in pottery, which, in the absence of written records that we can decipher, is the safest criterion of date. But it must always be remembered that the periods are not separate watertight compartments; they often slide imperceptibly one into the next. It is not reported that Minos declared, *I'm tired of Middle Minoan III, let Late Minoan I begin!*

The term 'Minoan', it should be explained, is a convenient one which is used to describe the whole of the Copper and Bronze Age in Crete. It is derived, of course, from the famous king Minos.

CHRONOLOGICAL TABLE*

PERIODS	APPROXIMATE DATES B.C.	EGYPTIAN DYNASTIES
NEOLITHIC	To about 3000	Predynastic and Protodynastic
EARLY MINOAN I	3000–2800	III–IV
EARLY MINOAN II	2800–2500	V–VI
EARLY MINOAN III	2500–2200	VII–X
MIDDLE MINOAN I	2200–2000	XI
MIDDLE MINOAN II	2000–1775	XII
MIDDLE MINOAN III	1775–1580	XIII–XVII
LATE MINOAN I	1580–1450	XVIII (to Thothmes III)
LATE MINOAN II	1450–1400	XVIII (to Amenhotep III)
LATE MINOAN III	1400–1150	XVIII (from Amenhotep IV)-XX

*The Table has been adjusted to the author's later results as published in his *Archaeology of Crete* (1939).

The positive dating is obtained by parallel finds of Egyptian objects in Crete and of Minoan objects in Egypt, for the later chronology of Egypt is now practically fixed.

Lastly as to further reading. I have already mentioned the monumental publication of the site – *The Palace of Minos* by Sir Arthur Evans. Less specialized – more general – are the late Dr. Hall's books, *Aegean Archaeology*, *The Civilization of Greece in the Bronze Age*, and G. Glotz, *Aegean Civilization*. Best of all short works is *Crete the Forerunner of Greece*, by E. M. and H. B. Hawes, even though it was written in 1909. [*The Archaeology of Crete*, by J. D. S. Pendlebury, was published in 1939.]

J. D. S. PENDLEBURY

VILLA ARIADNE, KNOSSOS, 1932

A SURVEY OF MINOAN CIVILIZATION

This survey was designed and partly written by the late Sir John Myres and completed by Sir John Forsdyke.

As the ship draws into the roadstead of Candia, there opens out between the Venetian sea-front and the sky-line of the 'Dead Zeus', on Mount Juktas, a pleasant landscape of limestone hills beset with olives and intersected by well-defined valleys draining into the open bays east and west of the town. Beyond there rise the higher foothills of Ida, snow-capped, to the west, and Lasithi to the east. This is the home district of Knossos.

Leaving the narrow bazaar-streets of the port, past the Museum, and through a wide breach in the eastern wall, the southward road sidles through the vast moat, and climbs slowly through mean suburbs, keeping clear of the eastern Kairatos valley, but crossing some small tributary gorges. A little beyond the inn, where a road rises to Fortetsa, a low ridge divides this broken country from an open basin of the main valley, the home district of Knossos, and the road descends towards the junction of two deep streams. Close to this junction, a low spur from the west slope below the road is 'Kephala', the 'headland', the site of the Palace itself. All this open basin is littered with the massive concrete ruins of the Roman city; the Villa Dionysus with its fine mosaics is in the high bank of the road; and the (modern) Villa Ariadne in its shady grove, a little lower, with the British School's depot, the Taverna, at its drive-gate. It was here that, lunching on the bare hillside, during an early visit, Arthur Evans suddenly exclaimed, 'When I come to dig here, this is where I shall build my house.' He had had a similar premonition, as an undergraduate, about his beautiful home near Oxford.

The slopes of Kephala are now clothed with cypresses and olives, and the saddle towards the high road is deeply filled with debris. From the south and from the eastern valley its slopes are still more abrupt, and the southern approach was by a massive viaduct, bridging the eastern stream. On the far side of this lie the 'Caravanserai' and Viaduct, and a little beyond them the Temple Tomb.

Though the Kephala spur has been somewhat flattened to form the Central Court of the Palace, and somewhat smothered by debris – nearly 20 feet over the 'Arsenal' on the north side – it still has much of its original form, and meanwhile has gained about 20 feet of stratified deposits of a pre-Minoan village.

Of this primitive settlement a few features have been ascertained from trial pits. It had huts of rubble and mud-brick, handmade pottery black or earth-coloured, stone implements, obsidian flakes, and rude stone figures of women, such as are found widely around the eastern Mediterranean. It does not differ appreciably from many other Cretan sites.

Yet the site had always natural advantages – a strong position, ample water supply, access to the sea and to a large fertile district with forests beyond. The food supply combined flocks and herds, some horned cattle, pigs and deer, with vines, olives, and figs, improved from native varieties, and fish, molluscs, and octopus from the coast. There were quails and partridges in their season, and ducks and geese in the marshlands. Skins and wool, and eventually also flax, provided clothing. The forest timber was far larger than anything the country now supplies, though there is still one grove of the 'Cephalonian pine' which furnished the Palaces with beams a foot square.

These early Cretans were already a mixed people, but the predominant breeds were those which have remained so through historic times. About 2000 B.C., however, appear the first immigrants from Asia Minor and beyond, of the thickset, broader-headed varieties which are found all along the great Alpine belt from Ararat to the Alps and Cevennes. There is not, however, at any period till the coming of Arabs and Turks, any racial segregation into classes or castes. On the other hand,

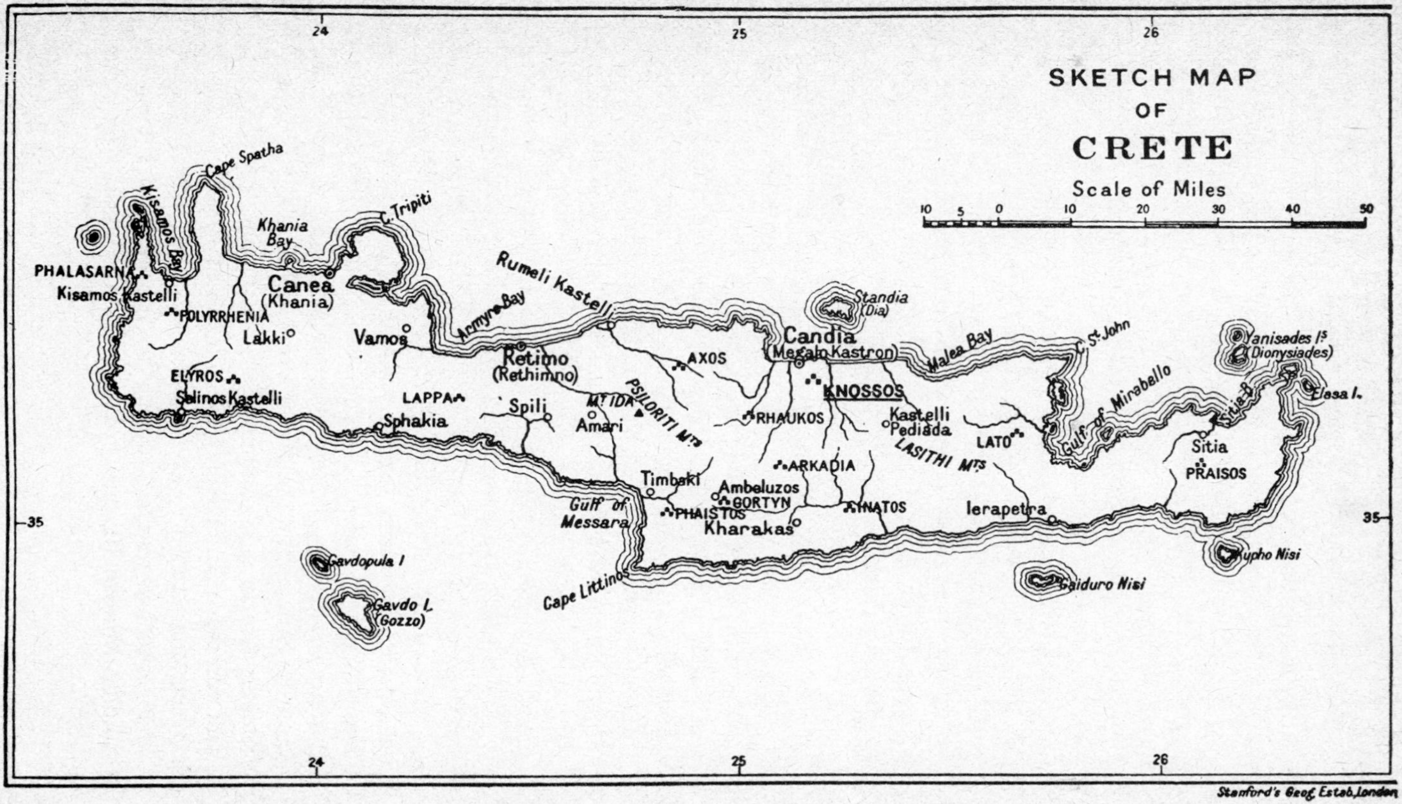

SKETCH MAP
OF
CRETE
Scale of Miles
10 5 0 10 20 30 40 50
24
25
26
35
Cape Spatha
Kisamos Bay
Khania Bay
C. Tripiti
PHALASARNA
Kisamos Kastelli
Canea
(Khania)
POLYRRHENIA
Lakki
Vamos
Armyro Bay
Rumeli Kastelli
Retimo
(Rethimno)
ELYROS
Selinos Kastelli
LAPPA
Spili
Sphakia
Mt. IDA
PSILORITI Mts
Amari
AXOS
Candia
(Megalo Kastron)
Standia
(Dia)
KNOSSOS
RHAUKOS
ARKADIA
Timbaki
Ambeluzos
GORTYN
PHAISTOS
Kharakas
INATOS
Gulf of Messara
Cape Littinos
Gavdopula I
Gavdo I.
(Gozzo)
Malea Bay
C. St. John
Kastelli
Pediada
LASITHI Mts
LATO
Gulf of Mirabello
Ierapetra
Gaiduro Nisi
Yanisades Is
(Dionysiades)
Elasa I.
Sitia B.
Sitia
PRAISOS
Kupho Nisi
Stanford's Geog. Estab. London

from about 1200 B.C., or perhaps a little earlier, there is immigration of northerly folk like those of the plains and steppes of Eurasia and the Baltic lands, with fair skin and hair, and light eyes; but these never became abundant in Crete or the Aegean islands.

The first great advance in Cretan culture came about 3000 B.C., mainly in consequence of new intercourse with Egypt about the beginning of the Egyptian 'dynastic' kingdom. Probably there was emigration from Egypt, which was easier than it appears, because there is a steady sea-current from the Delta along the coasts of Syria and Asia Minor, and thence past Crete into the Aegean and the West. Under the steep coasts there is also a daily land breeze and sea breeze, which makes coastwise navigation easy; and for homeward traffic there is a regular north wind all summer, and the return current eastward along the African shore. There was certainly very early contact also between Crete and Libya.

Of the earliest language, we only know that many Cretan mountains and other physical features bear names like those of similar features in Anatolia and the Greek peninsula.

Among early forms of skill common to Egypt and Crete are the shaping and drilling of hard and decorative stones for vessels and ornaments, the use of copper, the painted decoration of pottery, the use of engraved seals, and of pictorial signs for personal ownership.

This culture was called Minoan by Arthur Evans after Minos the legendary Cretan sea-king, and was classified in three main periods, each sub-divided into three. This arbitrary system – convenient from the first because every work of man must be either early, middle, or late, of its kind – happened to suit the Cretan culture unusually well, because there were in fact successive periods and phases of advancement, with their several characteristics. There were, however, also abnormal changes such as resulted from earthquake disaster at the end of Middle Minoan III, and probably from political crisis after

I THEATRAL AREA

1 SOUTH PROPYLAEUM

2 WEST MAGAZINES

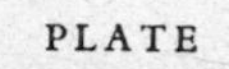

PLATE II

Late Minoan I, when leadership passed from Crete to the Greek mainland.

The earliest settlements are very much like the mediaeval and modern villages of Crete, close-packed groups of small houses of one or two storeys opening on narrow lanes or along the road to a port as at Palaikastro. Sometimes, as in the Cyclades, houses face inwards on to a ring-way, but there is at first no regular fortress-wall or protected entrance. But at Gournia a main street like that at Palaikastro leads uphill to an open space, levelled and widened by substructures, and on to this space opens a portico with one or more steps, and smaller rooms behind, evidently a place of assembly and administration. There are no large urban areas of consecration or ritual, though there are hill-top sanctuaries, as at Petsofa near Palaikastro, with votive clay figures of men and animals.

At Knossos and Phaestos there has been so much rebuilding that the earliest structures have been destroyed, and it is to the smaller sites already mentioned that we must look for primitive arrangements. On the other hand, at Hagia Triada and Mallia, we have the 'great house' developed independently of the primaeval village. In the maturer structures regular elements are: a central court, surrounded by principal rooms, and sometimes by colonnades and staircases; a main entrance with vestibules and offices; a range of 'magazines' opening on to a corridor and furnished with store-jars (this invariably related to the central court and principal rooms); a western court beyond the main block of buildings, with store-pits, warehouses, and workshops; private apartments with internal passages and stairways, not directly communicating with the central court. At Knossos and Phaestos, and probably at Mallia, a great hall was built above the main block, and served by a grand staircase: but these upper-works are only traced by foundations. The throne-room at Knossos, with its vestibule, store-room, and light well, is at present without parallel; and there are other rooms for special purposes, recognizable by fittings or contents. A few are certainly sanctuaries, with figures of deities or votaries, and ritual vessels; but these are small and secluded: there are no temples like those of the Greeks. Where the ground permitted or required changes of level, there were stairs, some of several flights; and there were upper storeys also over the magazines, the contents of which fell into them when the Palace decayed. The frequent reconstructions and additions have been traced in detail, and are described in this Handbook.

To determine the sequence of such rebuildings the associated fabrics of pottery are of prime significance. In the earliest periods, ornament is frequently incised, and the strokes sometimes filled with white earth or occasionally with red. Gradually incised ornaments are replaced by painted, on the clay ground or on a prepared black polished slip. This passes into the polychrome Middle Minoan fabrics, with their stately floral and spiral designs. Meanwhile buff-clays came into use again without dark slip, and made possible black paint, first dull, then glazed. After the splendid climax of polychrome black-glaze wares in Middle Minoan II, examples of which were traded as far as Egypt, Cyprus, and Syria, experiments were made in various shades of grey and brown glaze, with plain white drawing of great elegance. The disastrous earthquake at the end of Middle Minoan III was followed by a change of taste, from polychrome on dark ground to glazed black on buff, relying for its effect on stately but more conventional design, while fresco-painting still revelled in gay colours, natural forms, and animated scenes. This was the period of palatial reconstruction and culminated in the magnificent 'Palace Style' of Late Minoan II, brought to sudden end by the Fall of the Palace, and succeeded by various revivals and imitations in Late Minoan III, and a long decadence during a period of adventure and oversea commerce.

The first break in Minoan development had been due to earthquake about 1650 B.C., and it was in the period of recuperation that Cretan adventurers, and perhaps settlers, influenced the Greek mainland, during the rise of the new centres in the fortified palaces of Mycenae, Tiryns, Pylos, Athens, and Orchomenos, and the other sites where cupola tombs received the remains of chieftains and their golden gear.

Other Cretan adventurers settled in Rhodes and Cyprus, and made contact with the highly civilized people of North Syria, through the port of Ras Shamra, where the chamber-tombs resemble those of Cyprus and of Isopata near Knossos. Others again visited Egypt, and exchanged painted vases for glazed ware and scarabs.

In the history of the *Cretan script* all the main stages may be traced. As among most primitive peoples, ownership of implements and domestic animals is marked by linear signs, scratched or painted; masons' marks show the source or the destination of blocks, and became numerous and varied while the earlier Palaces were rising (Middle Minoan II–III). As the same marks occur at Knossos and at Phaestos, they point to organized and mobile groups of craftsmen. Meanwhile, the style and significance of engraved designs on personal sealstones matured, and the grouping of such signs showed that they represented syllables and formed words, probably their owners' names. Simplified linear versions of such pictorial signs were incised on labels attached to parcels, and as countersigns on clay sealings impressed with engraved signets. Eventually conventional syllabaries of such signs were used for vouchers, lists, and other business documents on clay tablets, of two main forms: foursquare inscribed in transverse lines on one or both faces, and longer narrower strips, inscribed lengthways, recalling Pliny's statement that primitive documents resembled palm-leaves.

Of such 'linear scripts' there were two in Minoan Crete; *Script A* was developed out of the 'pictorial' and 'hieroglyphic' system, and was in use with local variations in many localities. The largest known series is from the small palace at

Hagia Triada, near Phaestos, and is assigned to Middle Minoan III. A few such tablets were found in a 'hieroglyphic' deposit in the palace of Mallia, about the same date; single tablets at Knossos, Phaestos, Palaikastro and Tylissos, and a few short inscriptions on stone libation-tablets and ritual bowls and ladles. A variety of this script was introduced into Cyprus, and developed into the Cypriote syllabary which remained in use in historic times both for a native language and for Greek.

The other, *Script B*, is represented in Crete only at Knossos and belongs to the last days of the Palace (Late Minoan II). The clay tablets were found, some in the rooms where they were stored, with fragments of their chests; others scattered among ground-floor debris as they had fallen from archive-rooms above them. These tablets are very much more numerous and elaborate than the earlier ones, and Script B has been reasonably regarded as a normal development from Script A. But the differences between them are now seen to represent a change of language. Large numbers of tablets, precisely similar in form and content to those of Knossos, have recently been found in Continental Greece at Pylos and Mycenae, in chronological contexts (about 1200 B.C.) which imply that the language must be Greek. The historical conclusion is confirmed by current linguistic studies of the texts, with the result that the passing of Knossos and its empire to Hellenic control must be placed about the year 1450, two generations before the destruction of the Palace.

The Minoan artistic genius was inspired by natural forms, and its presentation of them was unique in the ancient world. There was on the one hand a strong decorative instinct tending at times to fantasy, on the other the desire to interpret nature in terms of its underlying character and life. The decorative quality is displayed in the long series of painted pottery, the commonest and best preserved of all artistic material. Progression there is from primitive formality to free naturalism, but always with a vivid touch of life or fancy. The subjects are mainly plants and flowers and creatures of the sea, together with conventional motives such as spiral coils. Exquisite patterns are made with rocks, seaweed, fishes, octopods and shells grouped together in realistic forms. Animals and human figures were not admitted to the ceramic repertory, but are shown in fragments of fresco paintings in characteristic movement and in more or less natural landscapes of rocks and foliage. The most sensitive studies of animal life are engraved on sealstones; works on a large scale reveal deficiencies in the technique of representation. Human figures usually belong to religious scenes, in some of which athletic contests, dancing, boxing, javelin-throwing or bull-fighting formed part of popular celebrations. Three black stone vessels, found at Hagia Triada and now in the Museum of Candia, are notable examples of sculpture in low relief, reproducing ceremonial processions and performances with complete mastery of the movement and behaviour of the various participants. Most successful in painting are the groups of spectators in the miniature frescoes from Knossos. Ladies of the court are drawn in detail as they talk vivaciously to one another beside a shrine. Impressions of the crowded populace are conveyed by brown masses of outlined heads, with white eyes, white collars, and some waving arms. The spectacle in one of these paintings is a dance of girls. Another may have been a bull-fight, of which the action is well known from a later painted panel at Knossos. At this one-sided game, in which girls as well as boys performed, the acrobat or victim stood in front of a charging bull, grasped its horns, and turned a somersault along its back, an athletic feat which seems to be impossible. If the performers were expected to be killed, the ritual would be a form of human sacrifice, of which there is no other trace in Crete. The bull was certainly a sacred animal, and itself a principal victim of sacrifice.

The Minoans seem to have built no temples for their deities, but several public sanctuaries have been found in open-air enclosures on hill-tops or caves on mountain-sides. They appear to have been places of pilgrimage, where worshippers could offer sacrifice or deposit votive offerings. Provision for religious ritual is also found in the palaces and private houses, but these were probably royal or domestic cults. There is only one representation of a sacrifice, painted on a stone coffin from Hagia Triada. Libations of blood are being poured by a priestess, to the music of lyre and flute, between two garlanded poles crowned with double-axes on which birds are perched. The blood is drawn from the throat of a bull which lies bound on a table. Other offerings are being brought to a dead man who stands at the door of his tomb, but the man was probably a king, and since kings were identified with gods, the ritual may be a regular form of divine worship.

The few religious pictures that survive give only a partial and superficial view of Minoan deities, which may to some extent be supplemented by analogies drawn from contemporary cults in Western Asia or probable survivals in Hellenic Greece. The objects of worship were the powers of nature controlling earth and sky and sea. They are represented in the forms of men and women so like their human counterparts that the deity cannot always be distinguished from the worshipper. Female figures are armed with spear or shield, or associated with the double-bladed axe, with snakes and various animals and birds. A young male figure is also armed with bow and spear and similarly associated with animals. These representations supply no evidence of the identity of the figures: they may show one god or goddess in several aspects, or different members of a divine company. Trees, poles and pillars were worshipped as the visible abodes of deities. The tall pole belonged to the young god, the short pillar associated with it would be that of the goddess, on the analogy of the biblical stocks and stones which stood for Thammuz and Ishtar. Pillar-worship had a material application in domestic cults, where main supporting piers in basements are marked with double-axes and equipped for the reception of liquid offerings. The deity propitiated there was doubtless the controller of earthquakes, perhaps the goddess whose association with snakes relates her to the earth. The young god was evidently the deity of the sky who brought fertility to earth, dying in winter and coming to life again in spring as Thammuz and Adonis did. In Hellenic religion he was identified with Zeus, but his annual death and resurrection continued to be celebrated in Crete, and became a scandalous heresy to orthodox Olympians for whom Zeus was immortal.

Many Minoan cults persisted in Hellenic Greece, and some names of deities, Dictynna, Britomartis and Velchanos in Crete, Hyacinthos and Artemis in Peloponnese, Athena in Attica. Hera has a Greek name, but her supremacy at Argos, a former Minoan centre, and her Homeric epithet 'ox-eyed' (or 'bull-headed') point to a Cretan origin, as do the spear and shield, snakes and birds of 'owl-eyed' Athena of Athens. But the unity of religious and social life in historical Greece was composed of many diverse elements, and those that can be identified as pre-Hellenic were not necessarily Minoan. The most certain heritage that the Greeks received from Crete was artistic capacity and the technical accomplishment which directed its expression.

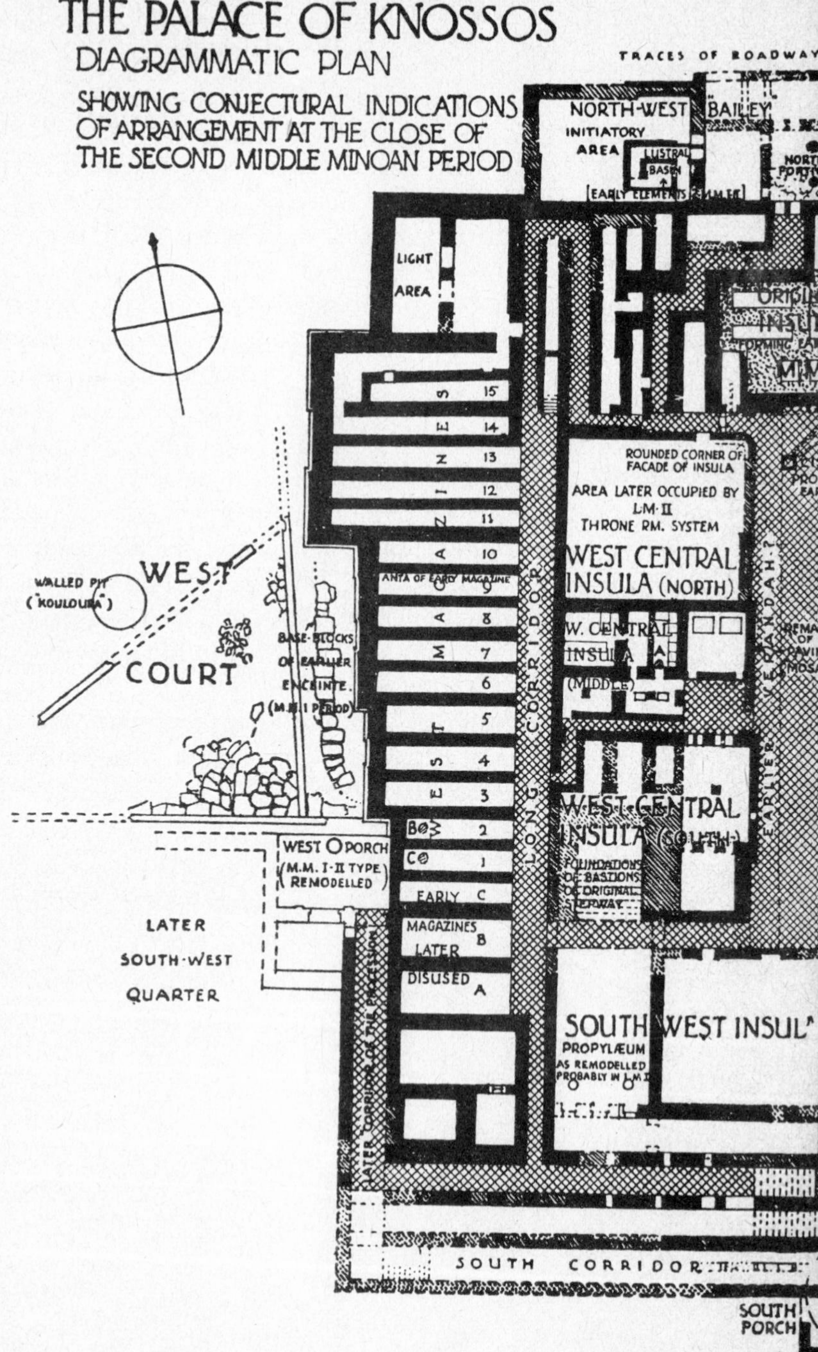
THE PALACE OF KNOSSOS
DIAGRAMMATIC PLAN
SHOWING CONJECTURAL INDICATIONS OF ARRANGEMENT AT THE CLOSE OF THE SECOND MIDDLE MINOAN PERIOD
TRACES OF ROADWAY
NORTH-WEST
INITIATORY AREA
LUSTRAL BASIN
BAILEY
LIGHT AREA
WEST MAGAZINES
ANTA OF EARLY MAGAZINE
WALLED PIT ("KOULOURA")
WEST
COURT
BASE-BLOCKS OF EARLIER ENCEINTE. (M.M. I PERIOD)
WEST PORCH (M.M. I-II TYPE REMODELLED)
EARLY MAGAZINES LATER DISUSED
LATER SOUTH-WEST QUARTER
LONG CORRIDOR
ROUNDED CORNER OF FACADE OF INSULA
AREA LATER OCCUPIED BY L.M. II THRONE RM. SYSTEM
WEST CENTRAL INSULA (NORTH)
W. CENTRAL INSULA (MIDDLE)
WEST CENTRAL INSULA (SOUTH)
FOUNDATIONS OF BASTIONS OF ORIGINAL STEPWAY
SOUTH PROPYLÆUM AS REMODELLED PROBABLY IN L.M. I
SOUTH WEST INSUL
SOUTH CORRIDOR
SOUTH PORCH
10
20
30
40
50
2 DIAGRAMMATIC PLAN OF THE PALAC

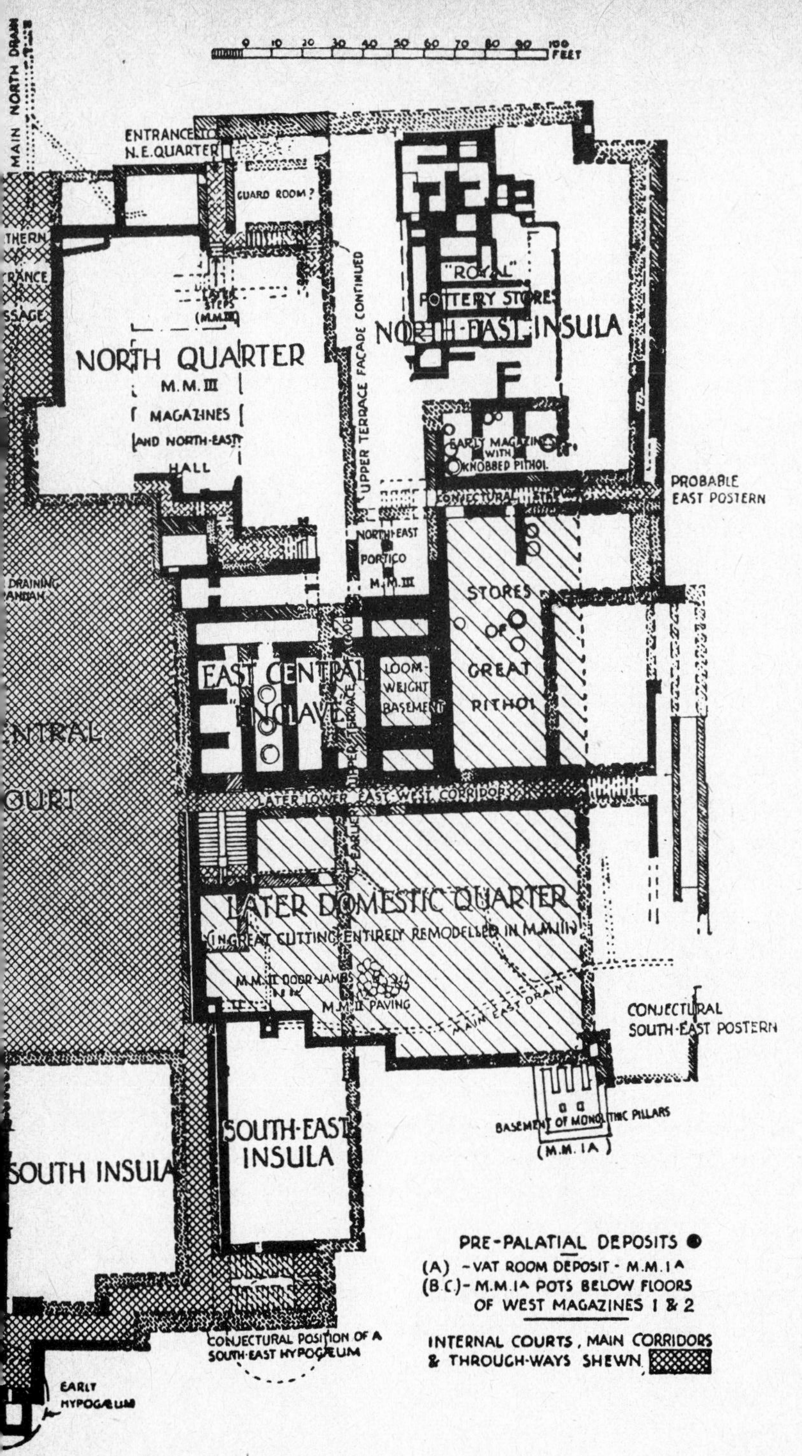
0 10 20 30 40 50 60 70 80 90 100 FEET
MAIN NORTH DRAIN
ENTRANCE N.E. QUARTER
GUARD ROOM ?
LATER STEPS (M.M.III)
NORTH QUARTER
M.M. III
MAGAZINES
AND NORTH-EAST
HALL
UPPER TERRACE FACADE CONTINUED
"ROYAL" POTTERY STORES
NORTH-EAST INSULA
EARLY MAGAZINES WITH KNOBBED PITHOI
CONJECTURAL STEPS
PROBABLE EAST POSTERN
NORTH-EAST PORTICO M.M. III
STORES OF GREAT PITHOI
EAST CENTRAL "ENCLAVE"
LOOM-WEIGHT BASEMENT
UPPER TERRACE FACADE
LATER LOWER EAST-WEST CORRIDOR
EARLIER
LATER DOMESTIC QUARTER
(IN GREAT CUTTING ENTIRELY REMODELLED IN M.M.III)
M.M. II DOOR JAMBS
M.M. II PAVING
MAIN EAST DRAIN
CONJECTURAL SOUTH-EAST POSTERN
BASEMENT OF MONOLITHIC PILLARS
(M.M. IA)
SOUTH-EAST INSULA
SOUTH INSULA
CONJECTURAL POSITION OF A SOUTH-EAST HYPOGÆUM
EARLY HYPOGÆUM
PRE-PALATIAL DEPOSITS
(A) - VAT ROOM DEPOSIT - M.M. IA
(B.C.) - M.M. IA POTS BELOW FLOORS OF WEST MAGAZINES 1 & 2
INTERNAL COURTS, MAIN CORRIDORS & THROUGH-WAYS SHEWN
DRAINING VERANDAH
CENTRAL COURT

T THE END OF MIDDLE MINOAN II

AN ARCHITECTURAL HISTORY OF THE PALACE

The Palace of Knossos is not an artistic unity. As a Greek temple reveals the spirit of a people caught at a particular moment, so the Palace, like a Gothic cathedral or the temples of Karnak and Luxor, reveals the history and progress of its builders. Older structures are adapted to a new plan; old foundations, once built over, lie in what at first seems a confusing labyrinth where the spade has uncovered them. It must always be borne in mind, as a main cause of this multiple stratification, that Knossos lies in what, as far as human records go back, has always been a great seismic centre. Earthquake after earthquake laid the Palace low; always it rose again from its ruins more magnificent until that final disaster from which there was no recovery.

NEOLITHIC

In the Late Stone Age the low hill of Knossos was covered by a considerable settlement, traces of which are found lying to a great depth even beyond the present limits of the Palace.

Magnificently placed as Knossos is today, it was at that time, before centuries of occupation had raised the level of the ground, merely a very low knoll lying in a trough in the hills some three miles from the sea (map, page 15). Ideal as the site was in later days when it looked towards the mainland of Greece and the islands, it is hard to explain its choice by inhabitants whose sole foreign connexion was with Egypt to the far south. on any other theory than that they were as indigenous as any race can claim to be.

However that may be, Neolithic Knossos had a long and prosperous history and was certainly the largest and most important settlement of its time in Europe and the Near East.

The houses were mainly rectangular in plan, originally perhaps of the 'but-and-ben' type, but with a considerable number of rooms opening off the main chambers. The base of the walls was rough stone-work; the upper part may have been of sundried brick. The floors were paved with pebbles or clay and red earth, and there was a fixed hearth of clay and small stones.

EARLY MINOAN I

The first part of the Early Minoan I Period at Knossos is really to be described as 'sub-neolithic'. The apparently simultaneous introduction of copper to the island from Anatolia and Egypt, and the resulting step forward in culture, took time to reach Knossos, which is hence throughout this period a little behind the east and south. One had almost said throughout the whole of the Early Minoan epoch; but this may be a misjudgment, for, as we shall see, much of the Early Minoan settlement was swept away when the first Palace was built. The few houses found below the Central Court still show in their contents stronger connexions with the Nile Valley than with Anatolia.

EARLY MINOAN II

Of the Early Minoan II Period only one house has been excavated at Knossos (to the south of the Palace). We have, however, a very good idea of the architecture of the period from the houses cleared by the late R. B. Seager at Vasiliki in the east of Crete. The houses were rectangular, possibly two or three stories high. Above a stone base the walls were constructed of sundried bricks tied together vertically and horizontally with wooden beams. The whole was covered with rough lime plaster and a fine surface wash of deep red, which formed a stucco as hard as cement and was really a structural feature.

EARLY MINOAN III

It is in the Early Minoan III Period that we begin to find traces of monumental work. While the houses probably remained of much the same type as those of E.M. II, there appeared below what was later the South Porch of the Palace a great Hypogaeum, cut in the soft rock, some eight metres in diameter, curving up to a beehive vault about sixteen metres in height. Into it a winding stairway descended round the outside, leaving windows at intervals to look into the vault. It is possible that there may have been an exit from the floor of the Hypogaeum via a tunnel to the sloping hillside to the south, the whole forming an elaborate entrance system. Such an entrance implies something behind it worth guarding, and it therefore seems likely that there was already at this period the nucleus of the system of *Insulae* to be described below which were soon to be combined into the First Palace.

MIDDLE MINOAN I

To the very beginning of Middle Minoan I can be dated the foundation of the Palace proper at Knossos. The top of the hill was levelled into a great Central Court by sweeping away such Early Minoan structures as may have stood there and raising, by means of the debris, the north-west corner of the site, where the foundation walls of small neat stones may be seen. To the north lay a long, narrow, paved court, which can now be seen projecting at either end of the Theatral Area. To the west also lay a court terraced up by the great wall which is the westernmost limit of the site. After a short time a ramp was constructed leading up to the court from the west, and, from the entrance so formed, two causeways ran across the court, one diagonally towards the north-east, the other due east to some entrance leading direct to the Central Court, past the piers of the early magazines which are still to be seen. A number of buildings, however, stood within the West Court, their basements sunk well down into the made earth inside the retaining wall. The court itself may well have stretched farther south, as far, in fact, as the heavy double wall of thick slabs which runs east and west abutting on to the present West Porch which probably lay farther back to the south. The West Entrance of those days faced west and was approached by a causeway leading from an outer entrance in the Western Enceinte Wall along the façade of the Palace. The West façade of the actual Palace itself projected beyond the present limits. Its foundations may be seen continuing the line from farther north and curving in eastwards under the present façade.

The Palace itself seems to have consisted of a number of 'Insulae' which were practically independent and must have given the appearance of fortified blocks. A typical example is the 'Early Keep' to the west of the Northern Entrance. It was irregular in shape, with rounded corners, and seems to have been completely isolated. Its east wall follows the line of the later west wall of the Northern Entrance. Within this 'Keep' were six deep walled cells, called locally 'the Prisons', running down some seven or eight metres.

Another similar isolated Insula would seem to have existed to the west of the Central Court over the area now occupied by the Throne Room system. The north-east corner of this system has a rounded corner similar to those of the Keep and to that in the West Court. Other Insulae were probably grouped round the Central Court. Many of the present corridors may mark the sites of older passage-ways open to the sky.

To the east the Palace seems to have sloped down in a series of narrow terraces to the great East Wall, visible at intervals below the Magazine of the Giant Pithoi and below the Hall of the Double Axes.

The latter half of Middle Minoan I showed many notable alterations. The West Façade of the Palace was pushed back at its southern end and probably generally remodelled. It is to this period that the main features of the present façade with its gypsum orthostates belongs, the early entrance direct to the Central Court being blocked. To this period, also, belongs the terrace walling of the South Front. But most important of all is the magnificent southern approach of the road which ran across the island from the south coast. This approach was remodelled in Middle Minoan III, but in its essential lines it is an M.M. I *b* construction. First the road is carried on a great Viaduct, which takes two short half turns to cross the Vlychià ravine; then it divides into three, one part to run towards the Harbour Town to the north, another to the West Court, while the remainder as a great Stepped Portico entered the Palace at its south-west angle by some gateway now lost.

The importance of this regularization of an old trade route can hardly be over-estimated. It clearly demonstrates the traffic which ran across the island and foreshadows the close connexions with Egypt which are a feature of the next period.

A particular characteristic of the Palace at this period was its elaborate drainage system. The pipes in particular show an advance on quite modern efforts which it is hard to believe. They are elaborately made, tapering towards one end so as to enable a greater head of water to drive through any obstruction, and neatly fitting one into the next. It is even possible that under the South Porch they may have run uphill, demonstrating that the Minoan engineers at this period had discovered the principle that water finds its own level. The incline of the section of piping that lies above the area which was occupied by the early underground vault cannot itself be regarded as evidence of this; but any conceivable access from springs in the hills around involves an ascent of the water.

MIDDLE MINOAN II

The Middle Minoan II Period is that of the consolidation of the Palace. The earlier Insulae were linked up and for the first, and indeed the only, time the Palace was a homogeneous whole (Plan 2).

In the West Court the early houses were razed to the level of the Court, their basements filled in, and the Court extended over the whole area, except where three deep walled pits, *Koulouras*, were sunk to receive the broken pottery from the Palace rubbish heaps.

To the north the level of the old North-West Court was considerably raised, and a broad flight of steps at the south side was constructed, on older foundations, to lead up to the causeway running to the West Porch.

Within the Palace the main feature was, as stated above, the connecting up of the earlier Insulae into a single system. The West Magazines were constructed. On the west side of the Central Court the old façade line was pushed back. The North Keep was filled in and built over; to the east of it the newly modelled North Entrance, with its full breadth, ran up to the Central Court, while a secondary entrance was planned slightly to the west, where the Lustral Area, North-West Portico, and the ramp ascending thence round the early Keep, were laid out.

To the south a porch was erected over the Early Minoan III Hypogaeum, and from it an open ramp ascended to the Central Court.

To the north-east the Royal Pottery stores and the Magazine of Giant Pithoi were built. It was the great age of polychromy in pottery.

But the crowning achievement of the period was the construction of what was later the Domestic Quarter, by means of a great cutting in the hillside immediately to the east of the Central Court, destroying the narrow terraces of the first Palace. Although this quarter was entirely remodelled in Middle Minoan III, the main lines are undoubtedly of this earlier date; for the supporting walls of the Great Cutting, the south wall of the South Light-Well of the Queen's Megaron, as well as the great walls of the Lower East-West Corridor are all datable either from the incised signs on the blocks or from the method of construction, with a clay bedding between each

1 GRAND STAIRCASE: UPPER FLOOR

2 GRAND STAIRCASE: LOWER FLOOR

PLATE III

1 NORTH ENTRANCE

2 DOUBLE-AXE PILLAR

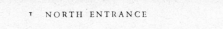

PLATE IV

course. The Grand-Staircase itself belongs to Middle Minoan III, but there must have been at this period something corresponding, if on a less ambitious scale.

The elaborate drainage system of this part of the Palace must also be referred to Middle Minoan II. The drains are carefully built of stone and lined with cement. At intervals gullies or minor channels run into the main system which is roughly oval in plan, its highest point being at the south end of the later Hall of Colonnades, the two channels rejoining east of the later Queen's Megaron and running out to some effluent to the east. Other drains of the same type have been discovered elsewhere in the Palace.

One of the most important pieces of evidence for the architecture of this period was discovered a little to the north of the Domestic Quarter. This is the 'Town Mosaic', a series of small faience plaques representing the façades of houses. From them we can obtain a very good idea of the domestic architecture of Middle Minoan II. They are tall and rectangular, almost towers in some cases. On the roof is usually shown an attic, sometimes with a sloping roof to let off the rain-water. In one or two cases the method above mentioned of bedding each course of stone in clay is clearly shown. The window frames are of wood and four or even six panes to a window are shown, with what appears to be some substitute for glass, perhaps oiled parchment. The absence of windows on the ground floor has been explained by the suggestion that they are houses built up against a city wall.

At the end of this period a catastrophe seems to have taken place, involving not only Knossos but also Phaestos and other sites. It appears to have been among the first of that series of earthquakes which periodically laid the Palace in ruins.

MIDDLE MINOAN III

The Middle Minoan III Period marks the beginning of a new era in the history of the Palace. It is in fact the Middle Minoan

III Palace which, with small alterations, is standing today. Several architectural innovations were introduced, such as the low gypsum or limestone column-base in place of the high base of variegated stone common in the preceding periods and the smooth polygonal slabs of 'almond-stone', the interstices of which were filled with red or white plaster (*mosaiko*), in place of the thick irregular limestone paving slabs (*kalderim*). Compact regular courses of masonry replace the older clay-embedded blocks. *Kasellas* or floor-cists are common. These new features taken in conjunction with a change in script and seal-types argue, if not a change of dynasty, at least a change of spirit.

The greatest changes are to be noticed on the east slope. Here the Great Cutting of Middle Minoan II was entirely remodelled on its present lines. The Grand Staircase was constructed and the whole of the Domestic Quarter is to be attributed in all essentials to this period. It may be as well here to note two of the peculiarities of Minoan architecture with which we have to deal henceforward. The first is the system of light-wells. These are particularly suited to the climate, not only admitting light to inner rooms which, in a building like the Palace, constructed on a slope, would otherwise depend on artificial illumination, but also shutting out both the piercing winds of winter and the intolerable heat of the sun in summer. The second is the downward taper of the columns characteristic of Minoan architecture. This, when one comes to think of it, is perfectly reasonable. These columns are of wood, directly descended from raw trunks which, unless planted upside-down, would be liable to sprout. Again, being of wood, the continual drip of rain after a shower would rot their bases if they were wide enough at the bottom to catch the fall. Being narrow, however, they are well out of the way. Lastly – though unless the column is very high this is not much of an argument – the part which has to carry the architrave is suitably broad, while the space between the columns, at a height where one walks between them, is appropriately larger.

Besides the plain shaft, traces have been found both of concave and convex fluting, as well as of fantastic spiral grooving.

The woodwork throughout the Palace appears to have been of cypress, a proof that Pliny's phrase regarding Crete as 'the very home of cypress' is by no means an exaggeration.

The walls, as has been said above, were of fine squared masonry, often backed by rubble and with the lower courses faced with a gypsum dado.

To turn again to the plan. The lower East-West Corridor ran farther east, beyond where it was later blocked, and led to some postern at the south-east angle, towards the East Bastion, in its present state Late Minoan I. To this period belongs the open stone conduit which discharged its water into the 'Court of the Stone Spout'. The area west of this gives clear indications of a great hall above. North of this lay the North-East Hall and Magazines and the North-East Entrance with its guard-room.

The Great North Entrance was narrowed at this period by the construction of bastions on either side, thus making the entrance passage the same width the whole way up. Outside the entrance the North Pillar Hall and the Propylon, through which the road from the west approached, were built.

To the west the Long Gallery of magazines was blocked by a cross wall just north of the tenth magazine, and to the south by a wall at the third magazine. The 'Enclave' thus formed is remarkable for the number of *Kasellas* or stone-lined cists which lie below the floor of the Long Corridor, and of the magazines thus enclosed which have the character of a treasury. Of a similar type are the 'Temple Repositories' containing the religious paraphernalia of some shrine.

To the north the eastern flight of steps and the 'Royal Box' were added to the Theatral Area. To the south the early broad Propylaeum was built with a typical *Kasella*, over which the wall of the present structure runs. The whole was paved in 'almond stone', and there was a dado of finely polished slabs of mottled blue-grey stone.

Just before the close of the Third Middle Minoan Period occurred a terrible earthquake which necessitated the re-building and restoring of most of the Palace.

In the West Court the paving was carried right over the walled *Koulouras*. The present West Porch was built and the whole West Façade was restored. The Corridor of the Pro-cession was widened and the South Propylaeum remodelled on its present lines. The Palace façade on the Central Court was pushed forward and the whole Court paved in limestone. To this period belongs the general appearance of this part of the Palace with the exception of the Throne Room. The large *Kasellas* of the preceding part of Middle Minoan III were filled in or paved over, and the same is true of most of the Lustral Areas.

On the whole, however, the construction of this period follows faithfully the old lines.

One point remains to be noticed. At this time begins the en-croachment on the Palace site of private houses. The south-west wing of the Palace (west of the Corridor of the Procession) is virtually abandoned to some powerful noble. The South House actually lies over part of the Great Stepped Portico. Most of the large private houses hitherto excavated were built at this period, including the Little Palace. Methods of building construction were substantially the same as before, but some shortage of wood is evident from the habit which now begins of making the jambs of doors from tall slabs of gypsum running the whole height of the door.

LATE MINOAN I

Late Minoan I*a* has left few traces in architecture. Towards the end of the first half of the period there seems to have been another earthquake. This was followed in L.M. I*b* by a con-siderable amount of restoration throughout the Palace, a notable feature of the repairs being the plastering of whole walls, to provide a larger surface for painted decorations, of which much survives all over the Palace.

LATE MINOAN II

Late Minoan II had little to add to the Palace, except the Throne Room system which forms a small entity of its own, and a good deal of fresco work. At the end of this period, which was peculiar to Knossos, the Palace was finally destroyed, perhaps both by earthquake and the sudden onslaught of enemies somewhere at the beginning of the fourteenth century B.C. The destruction must have been irreparable, for the spirit which had treated a continuous series of disasters as inspiration for fresh splendours was crushed, and the succeeding period only shows a partial reoccupation of the site. There is, however, no real break in the course of Minoan culture, and the Residency itself may have been transferred to some other neighbouring site.

LATE MINOAN III

To this last sad period belong the Shrine of the Double Axes in the Palace proper and the 'Fetish Shrine' in the Little Palace, where the columns of the Lustral Area were walled up so that their clear impressions have survived.

For centuries the Palace lay deserted except for the ghosts of its departed glory mournfully wandering down the empty mouldering stairways, the silence broken only by the crash of falling column or block. The early Greeks considered it haunted, uncanny ground. Though all round the area Greek remains lie thick, yet within the Palace, save for the foundations of an archaic temple, no trace is found. And with that wild spring day at the beginning of the fourteenth century B.C. something went out of the world which the world will never see again; something grotesque perhaps, something fantastic and cruel, but something also very lovely.

PRIEST-KING FRESCO PLATE V

1 QUEEN'S MEGARON

2 HALL OF THE DOUBLE AXES RESTORED

PLATE VI

NOTE

APPROXIMATE TIME TAKEN BY VISIT

The average time taken in going round the Palace by the route given is about 1½–2 hours. The outlying houses etc., *including the walk there and back*, take up as follows:

1. *The Little Palace	(passing the House of the Frescoes, from the Theatral Area) about 20 minutes.
2. *Royal Villa	(from the East Bastion) about 10–15 minutes.
3. House of the Sacrificed Oxen, House of the Fallen Blocks, *House of the Chancel Screen, and *South-East House	(from the south-east stairway) about 10–15 minutes.
4. *South House, *Stepped Portico, *Viaduct, *Caravanserai, and *Spring Chamber	(from south-west corner) about 30 minutes.
4*a*. High Priest's House and *Temple Tomb	(from Caravanserai) about 30 minutes.

Those marked with an asterisk are all very well worth seeing.

The whole site takes 2½–3½ hours, though, of course, much more might be spent on it.

For visitors with only an hour or two at their disposal one would suggest seeing as much of the Palace as possible, omitting the upper floors on the east side and, if possible, making the excursion 4–4*a* above mentioned.

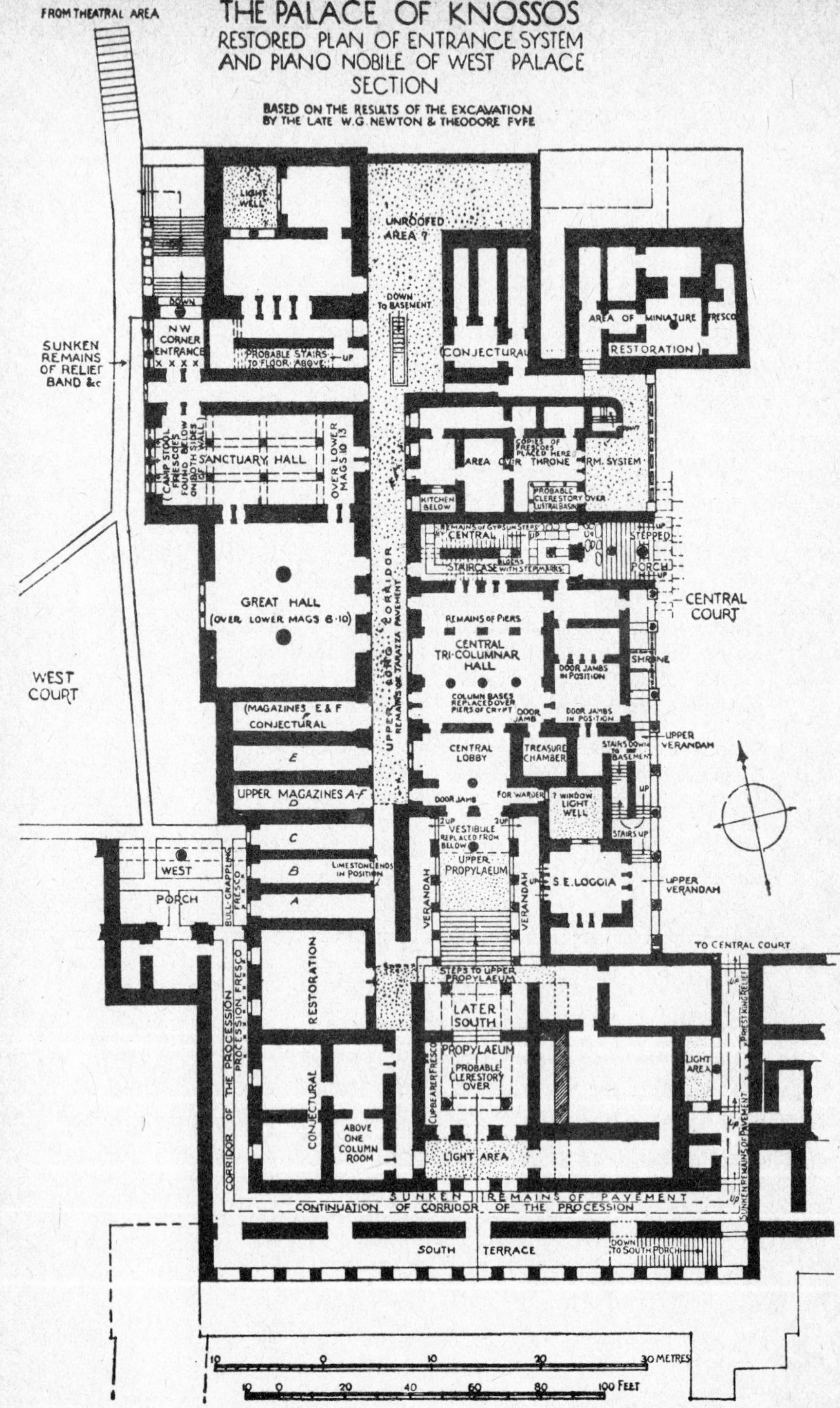

3 PIANO NOBILE OF THE WEST PALACE SECTION

THE PALACE

PLANS 9 AND 3

The Palace itself is now approached by the path which runs from the main road past the guard's house and over a modern bridge into the West Court.

This court was terraced up by means of a heavy wall, while to the right of the bridge you can see the approach that led up to it. When the court was first constructed (M.M. I, *c.* 2200 B.C.), the two causeways running across it from this entrance were laid down. One runs due east and originally entered the Palace by a doorway now blocked. The other ran diagonally across the Court to meet the causeway which skirts the West Façade of the Palace itself.

In these early days a number of houses clustered inside the wall; when the court was extended (M.M. II, *c.* 2000 B.C.) they were razed to their foundations and forgotten. In 1930 during the excavation of the two westernmost Walled Pits (*Koulouras*) traces of two of them were discovered, and the fine red-plastered floors and walls may still be seen at the bottom of the central pit (Pl. I).

These walled pits were constructed to receive the broken pottery and rubbish from the Palace heaps, and many of the finest fragments of M.M. II egg-shell ware were found in them.

In a room in one of the Late Minoan houses just to the north was a deposit of a whole series of vases connected with the worship and actual tending of the household snake, a discovery of great moment in its bearing on the primitive beginnings of the cult of the Minoan snake goddess. The 'snake tubes' here supplied for the shelter of the water-loving reptiles were themselves modelled on sections of the capacious clay waterpipes of the Palace.

Turning to the façade of the Palace it is interesting to see the way in which it reached its present form. The great foundation slabs of the façade of the first Palace (M.M. I) can be made out curving away at the south end under the present line. When, slightly later in the same period, the façade was pushed back to its present position, there was evidently some feeling that what had once formed part of the sacred Palace should not be profaned: an altar was therefore built in the deserted space to preserve its sanctity.

The present façade bears signs of the final destruction of the Palace. On one of the upright gypsum slabs you can see the mark where the end of a blazing beam rested, while all to the north is blackened by the wind-driven smoke. Now violent south winds are commonest in late April to early May, and the Athenian tradition maintained that this was the time of the year when Theseus sailed for Knossos.

Turning south you enter the Palace proper by the West Porch, with its single column and its guard-room and reception room where was possibly a royal seat. The decoration of the walls during the last period of the Palace consisted of scenes taken from the bull-ring. South from here leads the Corridor of the Procession, the state entrance. It is so called from the frescoes, on its walls, of a procession of youths and maidens bringing offerings to the goddess. This corridor, which now ends abruptly, originally carried on for some ten paces, then turned left (clearing the present restored south-west corner) and ran along the south end of the Palace until it turned again and entered the central court near where the Priest-King fresco stands (see below, page 49). At the point, however, where it breaks off you can get a very good view across the Vlychiâ ravine to the Caravanserai (page 68), the Spring Chamber (page 69), and the abutment of the great paved road which ran right across the island from the south coast, along which came the merchandise from Egypt, and Pharaoh's ambassadors to Minos (Pl. IX). The road ran below the Caravanserai and was carried along the huge viaduct whose massive piers can be seen, with steps between them to let through the water from the springs above. It then turned northwards and was carried across the ravine on a bridge. Here it split into three: one part skirted the Palace and ran north to the Harbour Town of Knossos, just east of modern Candia; one part seems to have entered the West Court in some way not quite clear; while the main division ascended in a great stepped portico whose foundations are still visible, to a gateway, now lost, in the south-west corner of the Palace, whence access was gained to the Corridor of the Procession. Nearer to the Palace, to the left of the approach, can be seen the South House (page 65) which encroaches on it.

Being unable to follow the corridor, you now go through the door to your left behind the red column, and take up your stand at the point where the guest would leave the Corridor of the Procession to enter the South Propylaeum (Pl. II). The south-west quarter of this has been restored; the remaining three column-bases can be seen. Originally it was wider, projecting farther east; for the sunk chest by the eastern anta runs under the present wall. The decoration of the walls consisted of a procession of young men carrying vases. The most complete of these – the famous Cup-bearer – is in the Museum, and the replicas set up here in their original position have been completed from this figure and from fragments. These figures show the ideal of Minoan youth, with their 'wasp-waists' – still to be seen in Crete – their long black curling locks, their kilts and metal girdles, the seal-stones on their wrists. They bear a striking resemblance to the 'Great Ones of Keftiu' whom we see in the Egyptian tombs bringing presents of Minoan works of art to Pharaoh.

The great pair of horns, standing near the Propylaeum, originally crowned the south front of the Palace.

Continuing through the Propylaeum you ascend the open staircase, which once was flanked by colonnades, to the 'Piano Nobile', the main floor where the state apartments and the reception halls lay (Plan 3). It may seem somewhat ambitious to have reconstructed so much when naturally nothing was found *in situ*, but the presence of column-bases and door-jambs, of actual steps as well as of paving-slabs which must have fallen from an upper story, together with the thickening of certain walls below so as to bear the extra weight, fully justify the attempt to make this most important part of the Palace intelligible (Pl. IX). In addition to this the disintegration of much of the lower story made some sort of roofing imperative.

At the top of the steps is a porch, and a vestibule, then comes a room with three columns, to the right of which lay a temple treasury, the marble rhytons and other contents of which were found below. The Upper Long Corridor which runs down the centre of the Piano Nobile was open to the sky. Not only did it have to give light to many of the rooms on either side but also fragments of hard waterproof paving were found.

Beyond and to the left lie the Great Hall with evidence of two columns and a narrower hall with six.

You now descend the wooden stairs provided at the south end into the Long Corridor of the magazines below (Pl. II). This part of the Palace must have been usually in pitch darkness; it can only have been illuminated by lamps or torches. Below the paving of the corridor lie a number of sunken chests (*Kasellas*) and the same is the case in the magazines. These had been originally lined with lead, and there is evidence that they had been used for valuable possessions. Remains of inlaid caskets and gold foil were found in some of them. Most of the great jars, in which were the wine and the oil which formed the revenue and the exports of the merchant-princes of Knossos, have been mended and set up in their original positions. When the Palace was destroyed some of the oil caught fire and the jars overturned. The blazing oil soaked into the gypsum slabs, many of which are still black and greasy.

There are eighteen of these magazines, not counting three at the south end which were disused. The truncated pyramidal blocks of gypsum at intervals are stands for the sacred Double Axes, which have probably fallen from the floor above. From upper offices must have come the quantities of clay tablets inscribed in the latest linear script of the Palace (Class B) that were found here, by many regarded as the most important find of the excavation. Over fourteen hundred of these were found, belonging to numerous deposits and clearly consisting in most cases of inventories of possessions and lists of men and women. These also contained graffito sketches of many of the objects referred to, such as various forms of vases, cereals, arms, chariots, and horses. Some of them were found contained in a clay chest, and from a tradition preserved by the 'Chronicles of Dictys Cretensis' it looks as if the first discovery of Minoan tablets had been due to a great earthquake of Nero's time, resulting in the breaking open of 'a chest of tin' at Knossos containing 'lime-bark' documents in an unknown writing. The Cists of the Minoan Palace were, as we have seen, lead-lined.

At the north end of the corridor you turn right, pass the small magazine where a large deposit of hieroglyphic tablets was found, turn right again, then left until you come to a wooden door in the blank wall on your right; you turn left again opposite this door and descend by a winding ramp. To the right of this are the foundations of one of the earliest parts of the Palace, the old Keep (M.M. I). Originally it seems to have formed a sort of isolated block-house, and down below the foundations run six deep stone-lined pits. Traces were found in some of a lining of hard plaster, which might point to water-storage. For dungeons also they would have been well adapted. When the Palace, as it now stands, was built, these pits were floored over, and from this area came the fresco known as the 'Saffron Gatherer' and the 'Miniature Frescoes' (page 47).

Passing through a door at the bottom of the ramp you emerge into the North-West Portico. To your left lies the

Lustral Area, now roofed in, where those coming into the Palace by this entrance could purify themselves by descending into Mother Earth and perhaps anointing themselves with oil, for small oil flasks were found here. It is in no sense a bath, though in the Late Minoan I Period they seem to have put cleanliness before godliness, and to have filled up most of the lustral areas and converted them into baths. It can never have been filled with water – the gypsum paving and wall-slabs would not have stood it. It is purely a ceremonial Purificatory Area.

Leaving the Palace for a moment you turn west to the 'Theatral Area' (Pl. I). The flat paved area has tiers of steps on two sides, and, in the south-east corner, a heavy bastion, perhaps the 'Royal Box'. Here, perhaps, Minos would sit to review his troops, to receive foreign envoys or the tribute from his mainland dominions, or to watch the dances we see in the Miniature Frescoes (page 47) while grouped around him stands his Court. Originally it was a flat open space, for the paving runs right under the steps and reappears behind them, while an earlier paving was of an even greater extent. (A block of one of the steps has been removed to show the various earlier levels.) Later the steps leading up southwards were added, and finally the eastern flight. The idea that this was the 'dancing floor of Ariadne' cannot be maintained. We must look for that below the East slope.

From the Theatral Area you look westwards along the ancient road, the 'oldest road in Europe'. It is well paved with stone slabs and on either side are cement wings and drains. It leads to the main road north (see above, page 30) and to the Little Palace (page 57), three minutes away on the other side of the modern road. But you must imagine it not as a lonely country lane but as a main road in a busy city. On either side lie houses, the House of the Frescoes (page 57) and the 'Arsenal.' The Palace was not isolated: it was the centre of a great city whose population can hardly have been less than 100,000 at a moderate estimate, if the extensive harbour town of which we

1 GIANT PITHOI

2 SHRINE OF THE DOUBLE AXES

PLATE VII

I CENTRAL COURT: RESTORED VIEW OF WEST WING

2 CENTRAL COURT: STEPPED PORCH AND THRONE-ROOM

PLATE VIII

have evidence is included. The road itself seems narrow, but we must remember that the horse appears very late in Crete and that the rich people were carried in palanquins, the stone-paved crown of the road being more of a causeway to prevent the feet of the bearers slipping.

You now turn back and pass along the north side of the Palace until you enter, through the foundations of a propylaeum, the hall with massive square piers known by us as the 'Customs House'. From here ascends, direct to the Central Court, the North Entrance (Pl. IV). When the Palace was first built, this entrance was the full width from the high wall to the left to the back wall of the restored portico on the right. Perhaps some fear of a swift raiding party from the coast caused them in Middle Minoan III to narrow it down by means of throwing out bastions from each wall. Above these bastions are colonnades, the walls decorated with reliefs in which we may perhaps see the origin of the 'Vapheio cups', with the decoy cow and the cowboys. That to the west has been restored to cover a reproduction of the Charging Bull relief which stood here. A staircase farther up the ramp leads on to the Portico. This reproduction is built up of many fragments. The leaves of the olive tree are in some cases painted in relief and in some cases on the flat. They show three colours, the dark green of the top of the leaf, the pale green of the back, and the red of autumn. The bull itself was standing when the Greeks came, for it was found fallen at a higher level than Greek remains. It must have lent some colour to the story of the Minotaur. All the Palace, in fact, seems to have been regarded as haunted, uncanny ground, for while immediately outside its bounds Greek remains from the Geometric period onwards lie thick, yet in the Palace itself, apart from one small temple (page 49), not a trace of Greek habitation is found.

It is worth noting in passing that the masons' marks on the blocks of this sea-gate of Knossos are in the form of a trident.

As you go up the ramp you see gradually rising the mass of

Mount Juktas where the 'lying Cretans' vainly said Zeus was buried. From some way farther west its shape is like the fine bearded head of a reclining god.

The Central Court divides the official and the state quarters of the Palace to the west (Pl. VIII) from the more private and domestic quarters to the east. When the Palace proper was founded (M.M. I), all the buildings which had once stood here were swept away and the present Court was made and levelled, the debris being used to raise the level of the north-west corner of the Palace. As a result, you now stand immediately on the Neolithic remains, which descend in some places as much as twenty feet. Traces of the paving of the court can be seen here and there. In the north-west corner, in an M.M. II stratum, was found part of the statue of an Egyptian official called User, perhaps ambassador to the Court of Minos.

The first group of rooms on the west side of the Court consists of the Throne Room and the other rooms connected with it, constructed in the last days of the Palace (L.M. II).

Fronting on to the Court is an antechamber with a stone bench on the north and the south walls, and a reproduction in wood of the throne in the next room, which has been set up where charred remains suggested its position. Next comes the 'Throne Room' proper. To the right stands the gypsum throne of Minos where it was found. Flanking it are reproductions of the crouching griffins, fragments of which were found lying here and on either side of the door into the shrine beyond. Facing the throne is a sunken 'Lustral Area' for purificatory purposes – not a bath as first supposed. There is every reason for supposing that this chamber served a ritual purpose – probably as a kind of Consistory for the Priest-Kings. There are signs here of a sudden catastrophe in the middle of some ritual of anointing, interrupted by the final disaster; flat alabastra lying on the floor beside the entrance together with an overturned oil-jar for filling them.

Beyond the Throne Room proper seems to be a small shrine

with a ledge, on which fragments of cult objects and ornaments were found. To the right of that is a small exhibition of pottery, while to the left is a room from which you can look into a small chamber with stools, a plaster ledge, and what may be a plaster hearth. We know it as the 'kitchen'.

The whole of this group of rooms forms a self-contained system, and it is probable that the king retired here for ceremonies that may have lasted for some days.

From just outside the north-east corner of the ante-room a spiral staircase runs up to the second floor (Plan 3). The rounded corner within which it ascends is a relic of the first (M.M. I) Palace which survived down to the final destruction. On the second floor have been reconstructed a terrace and a series of rooms corresponding to those below. Immediately above the Throne Room have been hung a series of reproductions of various frescoes found in the Palace and in a house nearby. Opposite the door hangs the group known as the 'Ladies in Blue' found on the east side of the Palace. South of the door is first a charming little work from the House of the Frescoes (see page 57) known as the 'Captain of the Blacks', the smart young Minoan subaltern leading his black Sudani troops at the double. Beyond that is the fantastic fresco the 'Saffron Gatherer',* the earliest example of pictorial work we have (M.M. II) (Pl. XI). It came from the area above the deep walled pits (see page 43). On the north wall of the room are two scenes from the Miniature Frescoes, which were found in the same area, though they are of later date (M.M. III–L.M. I). They show very well the impressionistic skill of the artist in portraying crowds. The way in which a number of heads and figures of men are drawn on a general red background, with splodges of white to show the feminine element, is very effective. Note also the excited arms flung up on the sky-line. The dance shown in one of the pictures is evidently taking place in some such spot as the Theatral Area (see page 44), for

*Probably in fact a monkey, not a boy as restored on Plate XI.

the causeways are shown and the spectators seem to be grouped in tiers one above the other. North of the door comes a very spirited scene from the bull-ring (see page 54) of which the Minoans were so fond (Pl. XIII). Both men and women indulged in this dangerous sport, and if the game really consisted of catching the bull's horns and somersaulting on to his back and off again, it must have required a great deal of skill and training. This fresco came from the east side of the Palace. Lastly come three more pictures from the House of the Frescoes. They are all studies of animal and plant life: the blue monkeys in the gardens and the singing bird.

Passing through this room and those beyond you come out into the Upper Long Corridor again (page 42). Turn to the left and then to the left again until you are on the landing of the broad flight of steps leading down to the Central Court (Pl. VIII). Before actually going down you should look at one of the gypsum blocks to the left of the *ascending* flight on which are clearly seen the marks of steps, thus giving evidence for yet a further story.

On entering the Central Court again you turn to the right, and on the foundations of the frontage you can make out the lower parts of the façade of a shrine (Pl. VIII). Originally there were two columns on either side of a central block, which in its turn supported a fifth. This arrangement is shown in one of the Miniature Frescoes (page 47). Only the slightest traces, however, now remain.

Beyond the shrine you descend a few steps into an open court – the Lobby of the Stone Seat. To the right of this is first the Room of the Tall Pithos and beyond that the Temple Repositories. Here were stored the treasures and offerings of the shrine. In one of the two big cists was found the famous faience figurine of the Snake Goddess with her attendant, now in the Museum. These big cists were covered over later and three smaller ones substituted, of which the central one is still in position.

1 SOUTH HOUSE

2 VIEW FROM UPPER SOUTH PROPYLAEUM

PLATE IX

1 LITTLE PALACE

2 TEMPLE TOMB

PLATE X

West of the open Court are two rooms with square piers in the middle (Pl. IV). These two Pillar Crypts seem to have had a sacred character, for not only is the double-axe sign scratched many times on each pillar, but round the bases are channels and containers for the blood of sacrifices or for other liquid offerings (cf. Royal Villa, page 62; Temple Tomb, page 70). North of the first of these crypts is a room known as the Vat Room.

You now go back to the Lobby of the Stone Seat and leave it again by the double-doors to the south. A passage to the right shows the piers of the magazines of the first Palace with the ✠ sign scratched on them as a mason's mark.

After ascending the shallow flight of steps straight ahead, you come to an open space which was later occupied by the Greek Temple – the only later building found on the Palace site proper (cf. page 46).

You now return to the Central Court to the south of the reconstructed verandah, which probably ran the whole way round.

Before crossing to the Eastern or Domestic Quarters you should look at the reconstructed entrance of the Procession Corridor (see page 40) into the Central Court. Near this point the Priest-King fresco was found and a replica has been fixed in its original position (Pl. V). This painted relief shows the Minoan ideal of a prince, with the waving peacock feathers of his crown and his collar of fleur-de-lis; who knows it is not some order of Minoan chivalry? Like an Egyptian Pharaoh he is shown wearing a much simpler form of dress than his subjects, a mere loin-cloth, in fact, clasped about him by a thick girdle. He seems to be leading something or some one, perhaps, as we see on gems, a griffin. And about him are the fantastic flowers and butterflies of a Minoan Paradise.

You now cross the Central Court to the top of the Grand Staircase (Pl. III). (The stone tower on the way is not ancient. It was originally three stories high so as to command a view of the whole site before so much roofing in had been done. It is now the architect's office.)

The presence of step marks on the gypsum landing block, to the left as you look down the first flight, show again that yet higher stories existed to the east.

The Grand Staircase itself is one of the greatest marvels of antiquity (Pl. III). Five flights have been preserved *in situ*, and, with its broad shallow treads, it must have been a fit passage for processions and pageants.

On the east wall of the balcony of the first landing has been placed a replica of the Shield Fresco, showing the great figure-of-eight war shields hanging over a spiral frieze. The original fragments were found in a space below. The markings on the shields represent the dappling of the bull's hide from which they were made; the yellow band down the middle is the bristly hair which runs down the centre of the back, as is shown in the Toreador Fresco (cf. page 48 above and Pl. XIII). The stitches for a double thickness of hide where the shield was most likely to be pierced are also shown. This balcony is known as the Upper Hall of the Colonnades.

Descending to the bottom of the Grand Staircase, you enter the Hall of Colonnades proper. The open light-well here is a typical feature of Minoan architecture. It successfully lights and airs any number of stories, while it keeps out the biting winds and the scorching sun, obviating the necessity of outside windows.

Leaving the Hall of Colonnades by a door in the north-east corner you go a few paces along the lower East–West Corridor and turn to the right into the Hall of the Double Axes. This has received its name from the frequent occurrence of that symbol as a mason's mark on the blocks of the wall to your right as you enter.

To your left is the outer Hall of the Double Axes, a large rectangular room the partitions of which could be separately closed (Pl. VI). There are holes for the hinges of doors, and it is extremely probable that oiled parchment was used to glaze the casements above the doors. In this room was found a spiral frieze identical with that from the Upper Hall of the Colonnades, but without the shields. It is reasonable assumption that in this case the shields themselves were hung on the walls, and replicas have been placed here. These, of course, would be of oxhide, and their curious shape is due to the necessity of having a glancing surface at every point, since the number of thicknesses necessary to offer resistance to a direct blow would render the shields impossibly heavy.

A wooden throne has been placed here corresponding to the traces of a plaster-backed throne in the next room (beneath the glass case).

There are two light-wells, and from the southernmost a good view is obtained up the ravine of the Kairatos River to the Venetian aqueduct.

Returning to the inner hall, you leave it by a door in the south wall which leads, via a dog's-leg corridor, into the Queen's Megaron (Pl. VI). This winding passage, which must have given a certain amount of privacy, is lined with tall slabs of gypsum.

The Queen's Megaron, also, has two light-wells, and, on a small scale, corresponds to the Hall of the Double Axes. Over the entrance door is hung a reproduction of the Dolphin Fresco, with its dolphins and fishes and sea-urchins. A frieze of dancing-girls seems later to have formed part of the decoration. One of the figures has been copied and hangs here.

The small room to the west is the bathroom. The bath has been considerably restored in plaster, and the curious convex fluting of the column has been taken from impressions discovered in the Little Palace (see page 57). A paving block has been removed to show the earlier phases, for the whole of this wing of the Palace was continually being altered or restored (see above, page 33).

From the south-west corner of the Queen's Megaron you

pass through the Corridor of the Painted Pithos into the Queen's toilet room. This room is lit by a small light-well, known from the masons' marks found there as the Court of the Distaffs. In one corner is a plaster base, while holes in the wall above, which connect with cisterns on a higher level, suggest that there may have been some system of running water. Against the east wall is the closet with arrangements for flushing, a connected system of drains and sewers and traces of a wooden seat. The elaborate drainage system of this part of the Palace is very well seen in the recess at the beginning of the dark corridor that you next pass through. The general plan was roughly oval in shape, the two arms meeting east of the Queen's Megaron and running out to some effluent on the east slope. At intervals there are minor sewers and manholes for inspection.

The room to the right of the dark passage, labelled the 'Lair', and now given over to the storage of pottery fragments, was probably a Treasury, while under the narrow stairway to the left were found the famous Ivory Leapers of the Candia Museum as well as other fragments which show the skill of the Minoan artist in such delicate work. Connected with the Treasury was the largest of the inscribed clay tablets found in the Palace giving in three sections consisting, together, of eighteen lines long lists of persons whose names are marked by the ideographs of 'Man' and 'Woman'.

The passage leads you again to the Hall of Colonnades, and again you make as if you were going to the Hall of the Double Axes. Instead of turning to the right, however, carry straight on and turn to the left into a small lobby, whence you reach the Eastern Portico of the Palace. Looking back from here you can see a large block of gypsum above a square pier. This block was projecting out of the ground before excavation began, and has been preserved in its original position. Behind this Eastern Portico are two rooms, one known as the Room of the Stone Pier, one containing lumps of Spartan basalt (*Lapis Lacedae-*

monius) which had been imported and was actually being worked when disaster overtook the Palace.

You have now left the domestic part of the Palace. All to the north was devoted to the craftsmen, the potters, and lapidaries. Looking down eastwards you can see the massive East Wall, a relic of the first Palace which sloped down in narrow terraces.

The next room, reached by rather a scramble, was known as the 'School Room'. It has benches on three sides and plastered receptacles by them. More probably, however, it was some potter's or craftsman's workroom, formed by building partition walls across a large hall. North of this is the open Court of the Stone Spout, so called from the spout which drained off the rain-water from the roof of the Great East Hall above and led it to the blind well in this Court. On the wall above is a fine example of a column-base in breccia. Its height betrays its early date (M.M. II).

Immediately to the north are the 'Giant Pithoi' (Pl. VII). These vast jars, big enough to hide all the Forty Thieves at once, are again relics of the earlier (M.M. II) Palace. Though they could never have been transported once they were *in situ*, they proudly display a multitude of handles and knobs to facilitate handling, as well as a decoration of rope-pattern.

You turn right now and descend to the East Bastion, where there is a strongly protected postern gate. The interest of this entrance lies in the elaborate method of automatically checking the flow of rain-water in the open conduit which runs down beside the steps. Instead of allowing the water to come down a plain incline, gathering speed the whole way then splashing over when it comes to a corner, the engineers led the water down in a series of small waterfalls; at the bottom of each it was checked, with the result that it reached the corner at only half-speed and turned it without spilling a drop. Near the bottom are two square basins where sediment was allowed to deposit before the clean water flowed out below. Sir Arthur attractively suggests that the Palace laundry may have been here. (From here to the Royal Villa, see below page 62, three minutes.)

On the flat stretch of land between here and the river – the only suitable space in the district – Sir Arthur believes the Bull-Ring to have been, the ring where the foreign tribute of youths and maidens, sent from the mainland dominions of Minos, showed their skill with the Bull of Minos.

From the East Bastion you ascend again past the Giant Pithoi till you come out on to a flat paved corridor where a grating shows the drain-pipes of the first Palace, with their carefully tapering shape to ensure a greater head of water driving through any stoppage. This Corridor of the Draughtboard was where the inlaid gaming table, now in the Museum, was found. On one side lies the North-East Hall, on the other, at a lower level, a series of openings with grooves for sliding partitions, which may be kennels, and beyond them to the north-east the Royal Pottery stores where the thin egg-shell ware of Middle Minoan II style was discovered.

From the Corridor of the Draughtboard you turn south. There are three openings. The left-hand, eastern one, is an open court in which lies the upper channel of the rain-water conduit which comes out in the Court of the Stone Spout (see page 53). The central door leads to the Magazine of the Medallion Pithoi of which several have been restored. They are mainly important for the light they shed on a particularly debatable point in the history of Mycenae.

The western door leads into the Corridor of the Bays, the massive piers of which probably supported some heavy weight in the hall above, whose general outline can be made out on the plan by following the heaviest of the basement walls. In this Great East Hall, there is reason to believe, a colossal female statue, probably the great Minoan Goddess, once stood, whose bronze locks were discovered below, as well as masses of charred wood. To this Hall must have belonged the series of high reliefs in stucco taken from agonistic scenes and representing the highest development of Minoan plastic art.

Passing through the Corridor of the Bays, you arrive again in the Upper Hall of the Colonnades. Leave the Shield Fresco on your right and, after going a few steps along the Middle East-West Corridor, turn right, into the Upper Hall of the Double Axes. Here the door-jambs which were found fallen below have been put back into their original position and a small piece of Late Minoan II fresco, showing part of a bull's leg, has been protected.

The door in the south-west corner leads into the Upper Queen's Megaron, passing the Queen's private flight of stairs. The arrangement of the rooms appears to be identical, save that above the Queen's Toilet Room is a room with a stone seat on the west wall and traces of a W.C. in the south-west corner.

Another slight scramble leads you south to a small passage off which open two rooms which have been roofed over. In this passage were found the Lily Jars, small jars of pinkish clay with lilies in white (M.M. III).

The first of the rooms opening off this passage is the bathroom, in which is preserved a very graceful bath decorated with sprays in the style typical of Late Minoan I *a*. On the rim are what look suspiciously like supports for a sponge-rail! The door seems to have had a low gypsum barrier and the room has been flippantly called the 'Nursery'. The second room contains three jars. One has a pierced spout, another has a spout, but it is not pierced right through, the third merely has the lip pulled out into a sort of knob. What an archaeological problem! How long did they take to forget how to make a spout? or, alternatively, how long did they take to learn how to make a spout? As a matter of fact all three jars are contemporaneous! The smallest has a pierced spout because it was small enough to be tilted to pour out its contents. The other two were too big to be tilted and were therefore carelessly finished off.

Round behind these two rooms, opening off the passage known as the Corridor of the Sword Tablets, from clay inventories found here, is a small shrine of the Double Axes. which has been roofed in (Pl. VII). It is a sad little building, constructed by men of Late Minoan III, after the destruction of the Palace. On the ledge are the plaster horns and rude statuettes of votaries, while in front are the tripod and the offerings. There is every sign here of a sudden catastrophic interruption of the ritual.

South of this is another Lustral Area and the remains of a staircase and a light area.

Looking over the wall of this light area, you can see, in one of the houses below, the huge blocks shaken by the earthquake of Middle Minoan III from the Palace façade. (For the House of the Fallen Blocks, the House of the Chancel Screen, the South-East House, the House of the Sacrificed Oxen, and the Monolithic Pillar Basement, see page 64 et sqq.)

Lastly, before leaving the Palace itself you walk along the South Corridor, into which led the South Porch, near which fragments of the old road can still be seen. Underneath this South Porch, in Early Minoan times, was a large subterranean vault, cut in the rock, some forty feet high, which had a staircase running round outside with windows looking in. It was evidently a secret or, at any rate, a heavily guarded entrance.

From here you pass along the South Front until you come to the south-west corner, whence you can either ascend back into the West Court or – I hope – go on south to the South House, the Caravanserai, and the Temple Tomb (see page 65 et sqq.).

THE DEPENDENCIES OF THE PALACE
PLAN 4

THE LITTLE PALACE (PASSING THE HOUSE OF THE FRESCOES), PLAN 5

The House of the Frescoes lies some eighty yards from the Theatral Area to the left of the ancient road. It is in the south-east corner of the cutting, and dates from the transition period M.M. III *b* – L.M. I *a*, i.e. *c.* 1600 B.C. The other houses are earlier (M.M. III *a*, i.e. *c.* 1750 B.C.). The entrance is in a small wing which projects north and contained, in addition to the entrance lobby, a door-keeper's room to the left. From the lobby are entered two passage rooms to the east, and to the west a long narrow room which, in its turn, gave on to the main room of the house in which was found the stack of frescoes. These thin fragile slabs of painted plaster had been carefully piled here in layers, and when, with infinite labour, they had been separated, strengthened, and fitted together they gave an idea of the brilliance of the decoration of even a small house. Reproductions of some of them are in the room above the Throne Room (see page 46). The originals are in the Museum at Candia. South of the Room of the Frescoes lie three more rooms, in the easternmost of which occurred a number of vase fragments decorated with designs of double axes.

Leaving the House of the Frescoes, you continue along the ancient road, passing on your right the depression which marks the site of the 'Arsenal' which has now been filled in, until you climb up to the modern road. On the far side of the road, just north of the village street, a flight of steps leads up the bank and thence over a small bridge into the Little Palace.

The Little Palace is the second largest building hitherto excavated at Knossos (Pl. X). It is roughly fifty yards by thirty. Much of the east side has unfortunately disappeared, including the actual entrance, but enough remains to show us a most

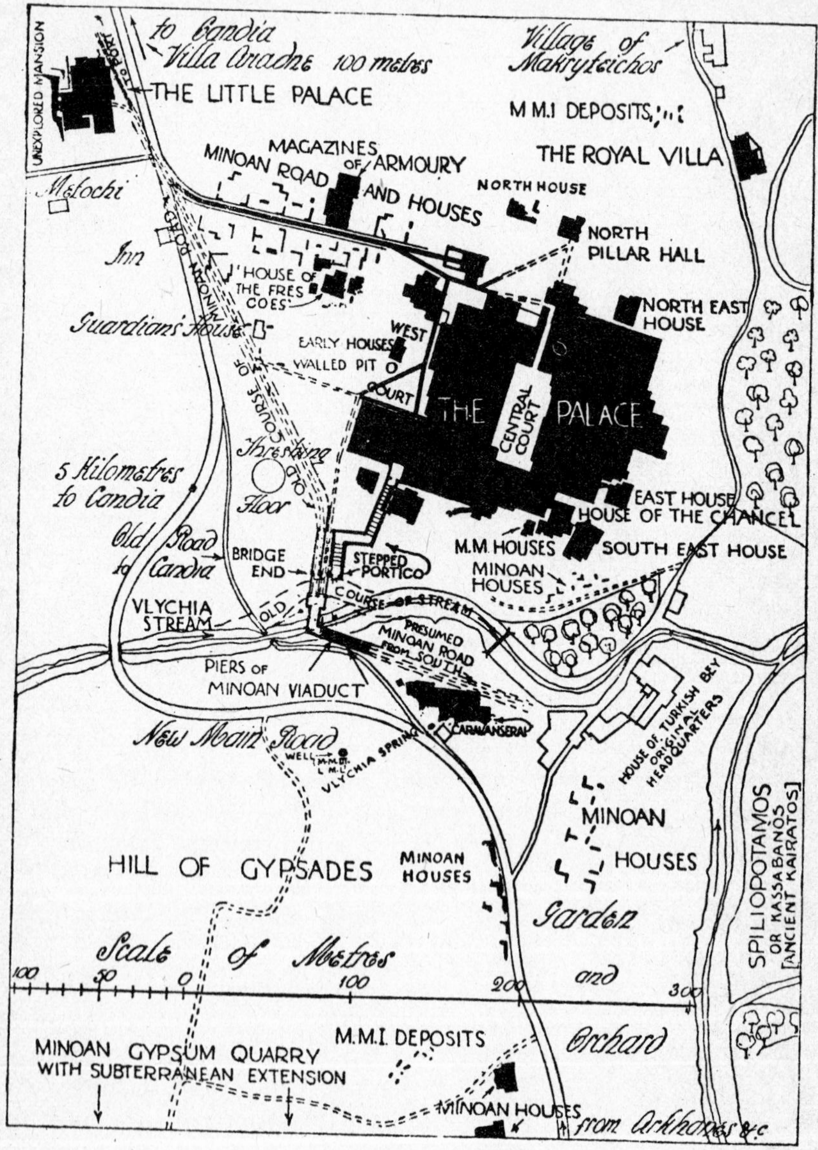

4 THE PALACE AND SURROUNDINGS

stately suite of reception rooms which the Palace itself cannot rival.

From the entrance hall four shallow flights of stairs lead up into the 'Hall of the Peristyle' beyond which was the Great Megaron. These rooms were bordered to the east by a corridor whose outer border consisted of two groups of columns between square piers. Whether there were further buildings to the east, or whether they stood on the edge of a terrace, it is impossible to say.

Off the north-west corner of the Great Megaron opens a paved lavatory with a stone sink. West of the Hall of the Peristyle is the stairway, two flights of which still remain. West again is a doorway whose jambs, instead of being constructed of wood resting on gypsum bases, are of gypsum the whole height, a symptom perhaps of the gradual deforestation of the island which seems to have begun about the period the Little Palace was being built (M.M. III *b* – L.M. I *a*).

North of this, part of the building has been roofed over, and is entered from the west. There is a step on which to stand in order to look into the Lustral Area. On the destruction of Knossos generally, at the end of Late Minoan II, the Little Palace was reoccupied by 'squatters'. They divided up the larger rooms by building partition walls, and in this case they walled up the space between the columns of the east balustrade. The wooden columns have perished, but their impressions remain and can be seen. It is from these column impressions with their convex fluting that the column in the bathroom of the Queen's Megaron was taken (see page 51). At the same time, the Lustral Area did not lose its sanctity, for it was used as a shrine, and on the stone balustrade were placed the 'fetish' figures of natural stone, the objects of adoration in the period of reoccupation (L.M. III).

Across the whole southern end of the building run a series of Pillar Crypts. The two most easterly lie at a lower level; between the pillars are the stone vats. The south-westerly

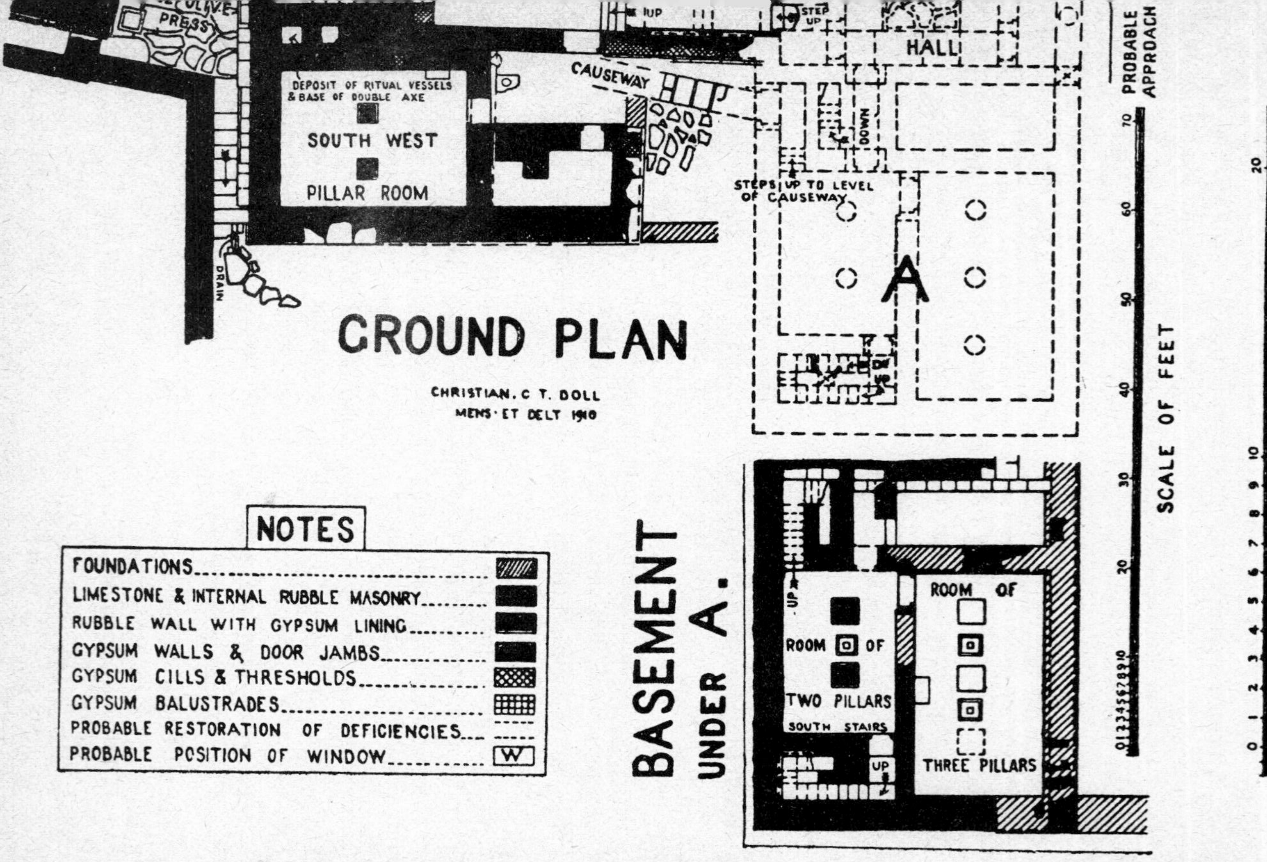

OLIVE PRESS
DEPOSIT OF RITUAL VESSELS & BASE OF DOUBLE AXE
SOUTH WEST PILLAR ROOM
DRAIN
CAUSEWAY
UP
STEP UP
HALL
DOWN
STEPS UP TO LEVEL OF CAUSEWAY
A
PROBABLE APPROACH
GROUND PLAN
CHRISTIAN. C T. DOLL
MENS · ET DELT 1910
NOTES
FOUNDATIONS
LIMESTONE & INTERNAL RUBBLE MASONRY
RUBBLE WALL WITH GYPSUM LINING
GYPSUM WALLS & DOOR JAMBS
GYPSUM CILLS & THRESHOLDS
GYPSUM BALUSTRADES
PROBABLE RESTORATION OF DEFICIENCIES
PROBABLE POSITION OF WINDOW
W
BASEMENT
UNDER A.
ROOM OF TWO PILLARS
SOUTH STAIRS
ROOM OF THREE PILLARS
0 1 2 3 4 5 6 7 8 9 10 20 30 40 50 60 70
SCALE OF FEET

0 1 2 3 4 5 6 7 8 9 10 20

SCALE OF METRES

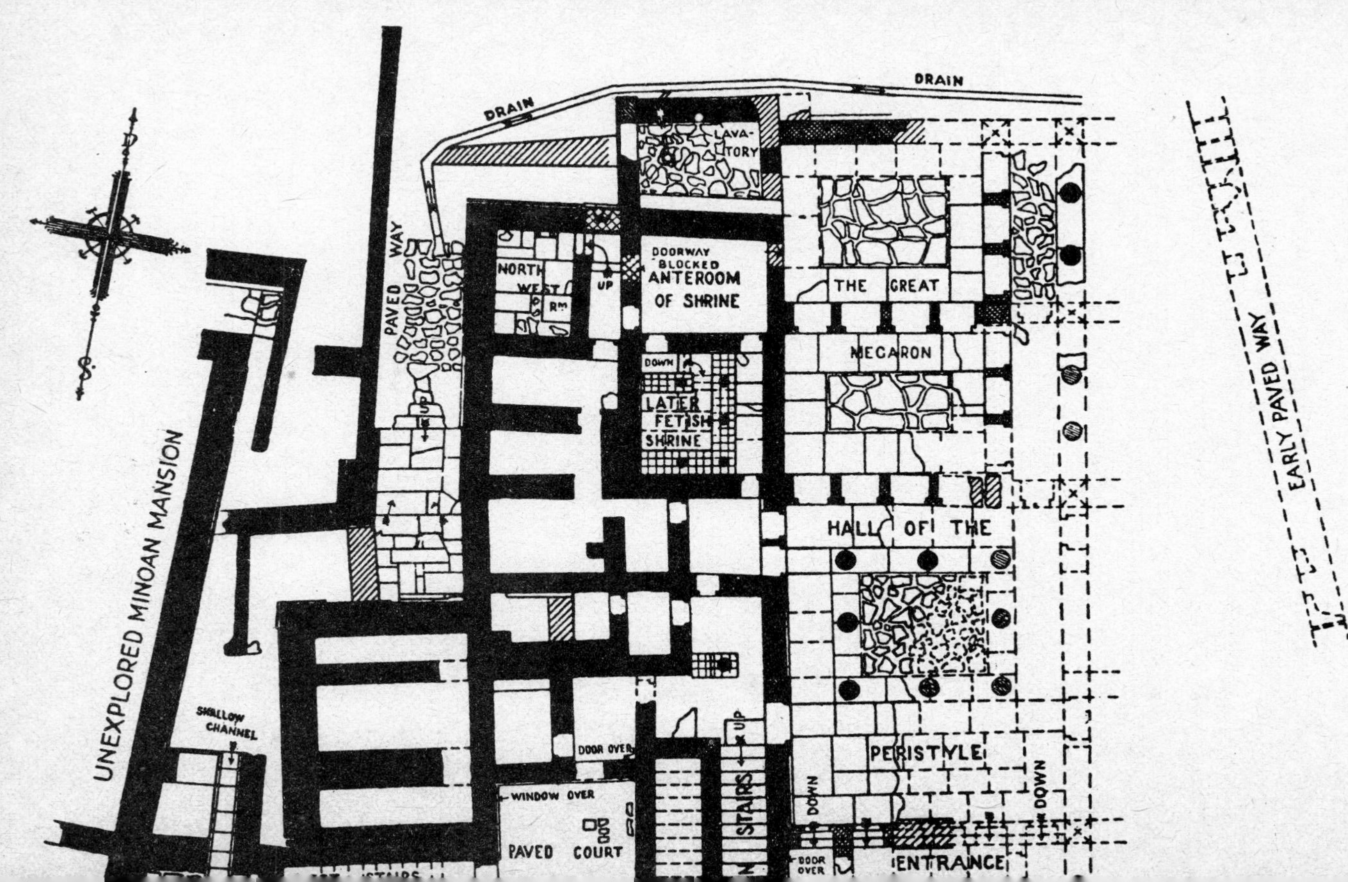

DRAIN
DRAIN
LAVA-TORY
PAVED WAY
NORTH WEST Rm
UP
DOORWAY BLOCKED
ANTEROOM OF SHRINE
THE GREAT
MEGARON
DOWN
LATER FETISH SHRINE
UP
EARLY PAVED WAY
HALL OF THE
UNEXPLORED MINOAN MANSION
SHALLOW CHANNEL
DOOR OVER
UP
PERISTYLE
DOWN
WINDOW OVER
STAIRS
DOWN
PAVED COURT
DOOR OVER
ENTRANCE

crypt adjoined a small stone shaft in which was found the magnificent steatite rhyton in the shape of a bull's head, as well as a number of other ritual vessels.

Separated by a narrow lane from the west wall of the Little Palace is the façade of a yet larger building, the 'Unexplored Mansion'.

THE ROYAL VILLA (PLAN 6)

The Royal Villa is most easily approached from the East Bastion (page 53). You follow the path to the left until it forks, then you take the lower one and arrive in three minutes from the Palace.

The Villa is set back into a cutting in the hillside overlooking the Kairatos ravine. You first enter a Light-Well, to the left of which lies the Megaron. Fronting on to the Light-Well are two columns, and the Megaron, entered from here, is divided by a row of three doors into two sections. At the west end, backing up against the retaining wall, is the throne, set back in a sort of apse behind a balustrade supporting two columns. In front of the throne is a lamp of purple gypsum. Above the throne was probably some sort of light-well, roofed over at a higher level, so that there could be oral communication between the seat of honour and the rooms above.

North of the Megaron is a Pillar Crypt with a single square pier, round which are channels and cists to catch blood or other liquid offerings (cf. page 48). From this crypt a flight of stairs communicates with the upper story. In the top course of the masonry of this crypt can be seen the slots for the great cypress beams which supported the ceiling.

South of the Megaron is a passage from which ascends a flight of stairs. As a matter of fact, the excavation of the Villa was begun by tunnelling along this passage and up the stairs. Ten stairs up is a landing, just above which was found a magnificent jar with painted decorations in relief, consisting of clumps of papyrus, belonging to the Late Minoan II Period.

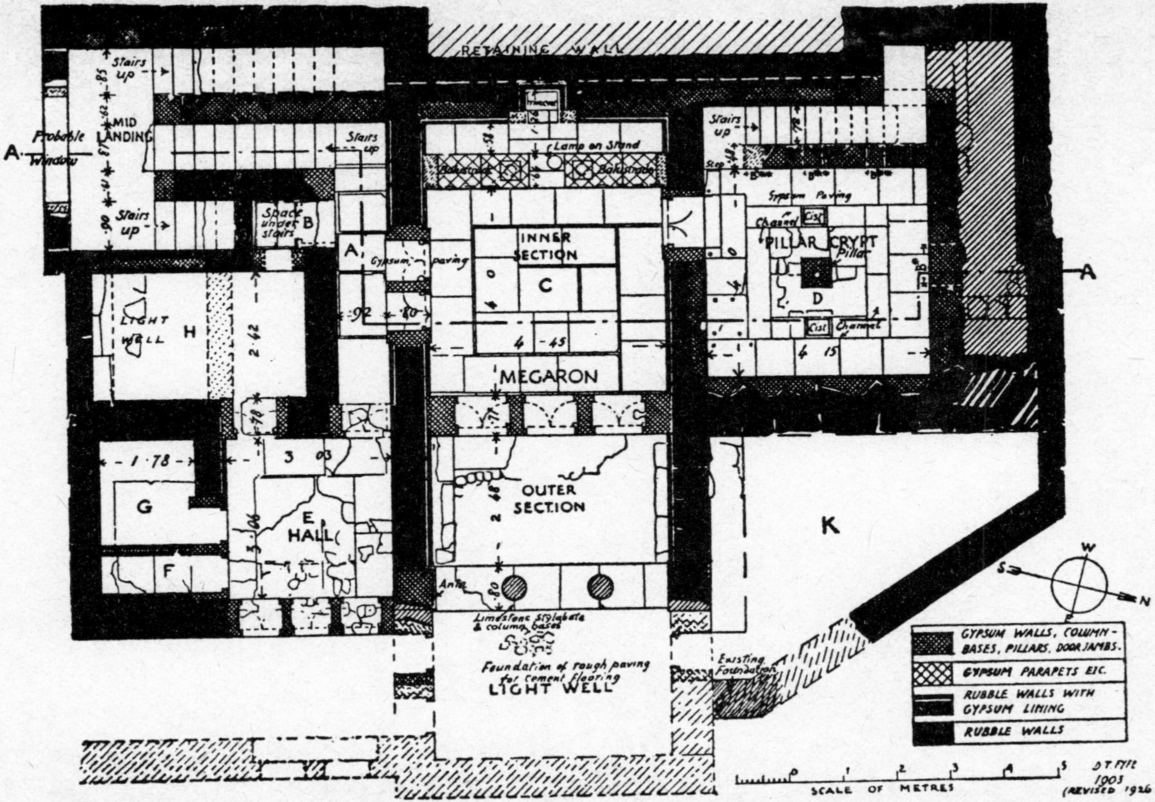

6 THE ROYAL VILLA

Above the landing the stairway divides into two separate wings to reach the upper story. This upper story seems to have followed the lines of the lower one for the most part, and it has been so restored. It is probable that the main entrance to the building was on this level, for a branch of the causeway which runs above the Theatral Area would, if prolonged, strike the middle of the west wall of the Villa. In any case, Sir Arthur is justified in seeing in it a dependency of the Great Palace of M.M. III date.

THE HOUSE OF THE SACRIFICED OXEN, HOUSE OF THE FALLEN BLOCKS, HOUSE OF THE CHANCEL SCREEN, SOUTH-EAST HOUSE

The first two of these houses are M.M. III constructions, overthrown by the great earthquake about the middle of M.M. III *b*. As a result, only the basement rooms remain. They lie just below the south-east angle of the Palace (page 56). In the first of these was found the remains of a sacrifice, a tripod altar and the horns of a Urus bull. Into the second house had been hurled a number of huge blocks from the Palace façade.

The House of the Chancel Screen which adjoins these has been partially covered over. It, too, seems to have been deserted after the earthquake. Its entrance has disappeared, but probably a passage led to the steps which ascend into the Central Hall, off which the Megaron opens to the north. At the west end of the Megaron is a dais for a seat of honour, railed off by a balustrade on which stood two columns (cf. Royal Villa, page 62). This has given the house its name, and even the workmen called it the 'House of the Priest' (τοῦ Παπᾶ τὸ Σπίτι).

In the middle of the west side of the house is a Pillar Crypt with one square pier; while close to the entrance is a small Lustral Area.

The South-East House you descend to from the House of the Chancel Screen by what may well have been its original en-

'SAFFRON-GATHERER' FRESCO

PLATE XI

PARTRIDGE AND HOOPOE FRESCO

PLATE XII

trance, two flights of stairs. At the bottom of these is a corridor, and to the left a Pillar Crypt with the usual sunken cist, and, by the wall, a libation-table. Beside the pillar is a truncated pyramidal block, the support for a Double Axe. The crypt was lighted by a magnificent tall lamp of purple gypsum, sculptured in the style of an Egyptian papyrus sceptre. The Megaron lay to the south of the House behind a peristyle, whose tall column-bases of polychrome stone show that they belong to the beginning of the Third Middle Minoan Period, if not earlier than that. The house is especially distinguished by the beautiful lily fresco which was found close to the staircase.

North of this house lie a number of buildings contemporary with the first Palace (M.M. I), most notable of which is the monolithic pillar basement lying just below the South Light-Well of the Hall of the Double Axes (page 51). It is a question whether these buildings ever formed part of the Palace proper.

THE SOUTH HOUSE (PLAN 7), STEPPED PORTICO AND VIADUCT, CARAVANSERAI, AND SPRING CHAMBER

The South House lies just below the south-west corner of the Palace. It was evidently built soon after the disastrous earthquake towards the end of the Middle Minoan III *b* Period, for, like many buildings of that date, it encroached on what had hitherto been Palace ground; in this case on the Stepped Portico which led up to the main entrance from the south (Pl. IX). Very likely this practice is evidence of the rise of the power of the nobles at the expense of the king. Enough has been recovered to render the plan of two stories and a basement, and the presence of a third story certain.

Though the original entrance was probably in the south-east corner, the house is now entered direct from the causeway into the columnar hall of the middle story. By the column is a stand for a Double Axe. From the north-east corner of the room a narrow staircase, lighted by a large window, leads down to the Pillar Crypt below. The pillar is not set quite square with the room. On one side is another stand for a Double Axe; on the other, three depressions in the paving mark the site of stands for other sacred objects. In the doorway of this room was found a hoard of silver vessels originally stored in wooden chests. The next room to the east opens to the north on to a lavatory and latrine, and to the south on to a hall with three columns. North of this a passage leads to the Lustral Area. The east side of the house was probably occupied by the entrance system.

Near the Lustral Area a flight of stairs leads down to the basement. The doors at this lowest level have jambs of gypsum which run the whole height and give evidence of a certain shortage of wood in this period (cf. Little Palace, page 58). It is interesting to see the primitive way of locking the door which is here adopted. A bar was slid across the door into a slot in the jamb, where it was locked by bronze pins which slid in through holes in the jamb above and below.

It is noteworthy that both this cellar and the smaller one opening off it could only be locked from within. Were they wine cellars? The main cellar has three square piers supporting the roof, and opens directly into the smaller one, in which was found a hoard of bronze tools including a long saw. It is possible that this latter room could be entered by a trap-door from above.

The Stepped Portico lies to the right of the path as you descend from the South House. It presents at the moment a most confusing appearance. Originally it carried a great stepped approach from the lowest point visible, where the bridge-head crossing the ravine ended, up to the lost South-West Porch of the Palace. At intervals the foundations are strengthened to bear the weight of the columns which supported the roof. These columns only occurred on the western side; the eastern (nearest) side rose up a blank wall. To the west of the stepped approach another road led up parallel to it and ran direct to the south-west corner of the West Court; while yet a third branch

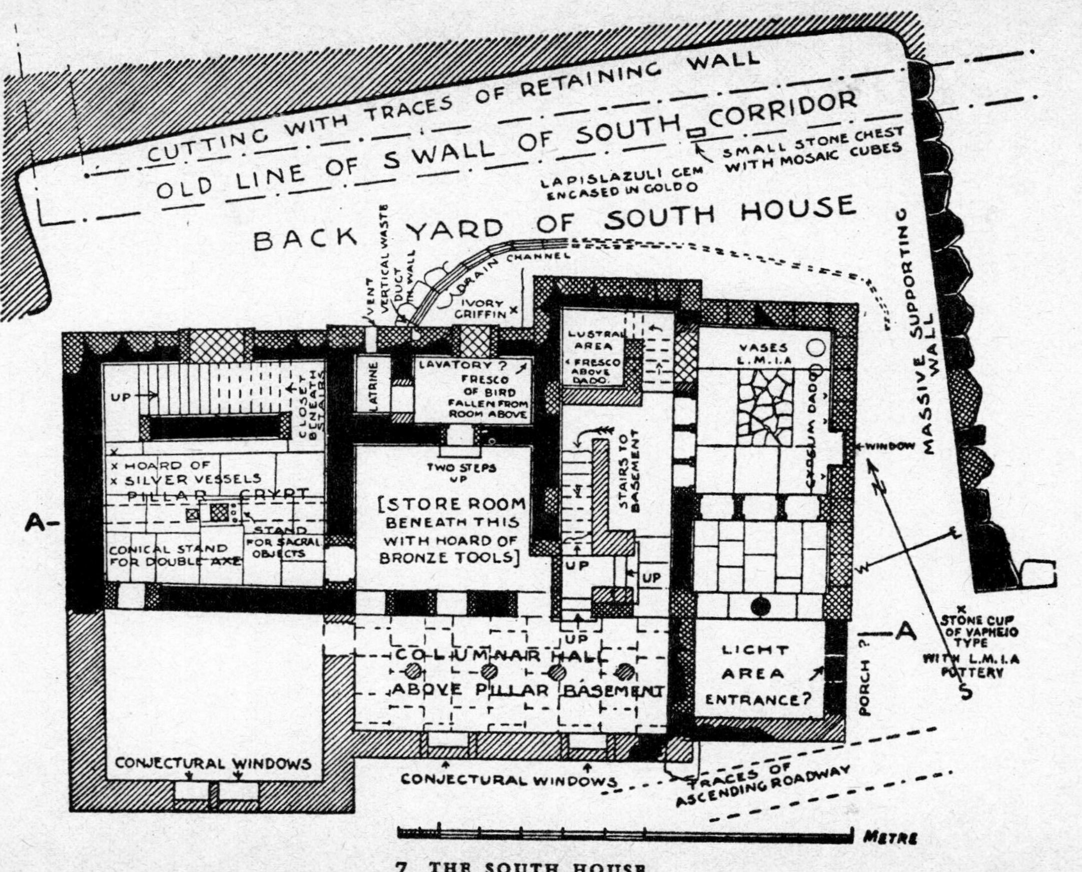
CUTTING WITH TRACES OF RETAINING WALL
OLD LINE OF S WALL OF SOUTH CORRIDOR
SMALL STONE CHEST WITH MOSAIC CUBES
LAPISLAZULI GEM ENCASED IN GOLD
BACK YARD OF SOUTH HOUSE
VENT
VERTICAL WASTE DUCT IN WALL
DRAIN CHANNEL
IVORY GRIFFIN
MASSIVE SUPPORTING WALL
UP
CLOSET BENEATH STAIRS
LATRINE
LAVATORY ?
FRESCO OF BIRD FALLEN FROM ROOM ABOVE
LUSTRAL AREA
FRESCO ABOVE DADO.
VASES L.M.I.A
CYPSUM DADO
WINDOW
HOARD OF SILVER VESSELS
PILLAR CRYPT
TWO STEPS UP
STAIRS TO BASEMENT
[STORE ROOM BENEATH THIS WITH HOARD OF BRONZE TOOLS]
STAND FOR SACRAL OBJECTS
CONICAL STAND FOR DOUBLE AXE
A-
UP
UP
UP
COLUMNAR HALL ABOVE PILLAR BASEMENT
LIGHT AREA
ENTRANCE?
PORCH ?
A
STONE CUP OF VAPHEIO TYPE WITH L.M.I.A POTTERY
N
E
W
S
CONJECTURAL WINDOWS
CONJECTURAL WINDOWS
TRACES OF ASCENDING ROADWAY
METRE

7 THE SOUTH HOUSE

skirted the Palace area completely and formed the highway to the Harbour Town three miles to the north (see map, page 15).

Of the bridge which spanned the ravine, apparently changing direction twice, nothing remains but the deep foundations abutting on to the Stepped Portico; but we know that it must have joined the Viaduct to the south.

The Viaduct which stands out boldly from the south bank of the ravine was, like the Stepped Portico, laid out at the time of the first Palace (M.M. I). The piers are still preserved up to a good height. Between them are stepped culverts to allow for the passage of flood-water from the hill above. These culverts were bridged over to support the roadway, probably by means of the flat-topped corbelled arches we see in Mycenaean bridges on the mainland.

This is the most massive piece of Minoan work that has come to light in Crete. It gives a very good idea of the skill of the engineers, as well as the amount of traffic which must have run across the island from the south coast even in those early days.

The Caravanserai lies above the Viaduct. The two main rooms have been roofed over. First is a pavilion approached by a short flight of steps and fronted by a single column. A good deal of the original painted plaster remains low down on the walls, while, in its original position above, a reproduction of part of a frieze representing partridges and hoopoes has been placed (Pl. XII). Contrary to the general opinion, the many-coloured round objects at the base of the picture are not hoopoe's eggs but stones! This frieze bears considerable likeness to some of the work from the House of the Frescoes (see page 47) and the two buildings are certainly contemporaneous (M.M. III–L.M. I).

Next to the Pavilion is a stone bath for washing the feet (Pl. XIV). It was fed by pipes with water from the springs above, and flowed out into a stone drinking-trough for animals, while an emergency overflow channel was also provided. The source of the water-supply has been restored.

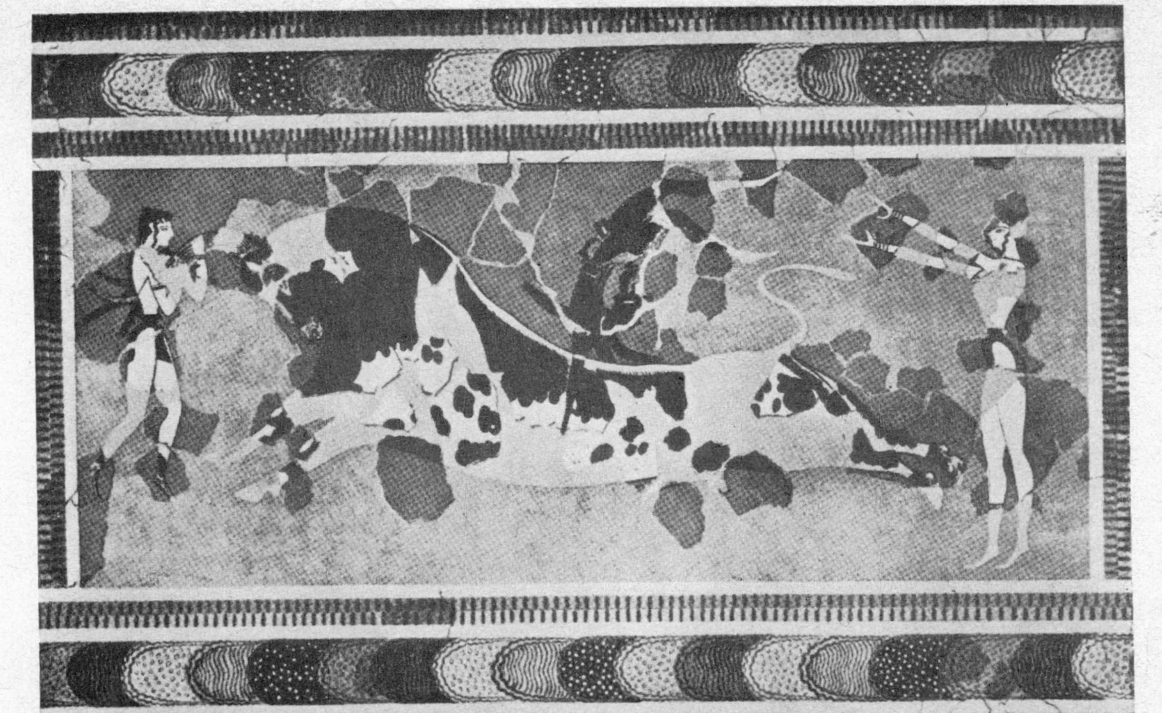

TOREADOR FRESCO PLATE XIII

1 FOOTBATH IN THE CARAVANSERAI

2 SPRING CHAMBER

PLATE XIV

West of the footbath is a room in which were found fragments of a number of clay bath-tubs. These, taken in conjunction with the deposit of carbonized particles in the waste-duct here, give the impression that the tired traveller could even indulge in the luxury of a hot bath.

The rest of the Caravanserai consists of small rooms and cobbled yards.

The Spring Chamber lies at an angle just to the west of the Caravanserai (Pl. XIV). Here the water in the basin wells up between the pebbles of the flooring. In the niche at the back is a lamp, while the ledges on either side were for offerings. You notice, too, the well-worn step in front of the basin. (From here to the Temple Tomb, see immediately below, 15 minutes.

THE HOUSE OF THE HIGH PRIEST AND THE TEMPLE TOMB (PLAN 8)

From the back of the Caravanserai you climb up to the modern road and turn left along it. On the face of the cutting to the right of the road you can see, here and there, the façades of yet unexplored houses, for the whole of this hill formed part of the city of Knossos. A little farther on, just after the road has turned, there are the remains of two houses in a cornfield above, which were cleared in the first year of excavation.

Some three hundred yards from the Caravanserai is a ruined house, just below the road and to the left. Here a path leads down to a building which was partly excavated in 1931. The bulk of this house is under the road.

The House of the High Priest is so named from the stone altar which has been set back behind a chancel-like structure, a balustrade supporting two columns. On either side of the entrance are chests for offerings. Flanking the altar are stands for Double Axes, one of which is a cement copy. In front of the altar a hole leads down into a stone drain which reappears below the steps in front. The altar space seems to have been railed off by a metal grille, holes for the attachment of which can be seen between the two chests.

The east side of the house has been destroyed: only a few massive gypsum walls towards the south end have survived. The steps at this point evidently led from the paved street, which was found some way below, up to a higher thoroughfare which brought this house into direct relation with the Royal Temple Tomb.

The Royal *Temple Tomb* lies some two hundred yards on (Pl. X). After passing a house on the right of the road you ascend a steep path up the bank into a vineyard, descending again immediately to your left down to the level of the lower entrance. This entrance leads into the north end of the Pavilion, a portico with two columns which fronts on to the open paved court. The antae of this portico have been raised to this height by the use of the original blocks which were found in a later wall. In the same way the massive pylons, on either side of the gateway facing the Pavilion, with the trident sign incised on them, have been restored by the recovery of the old blocks from elsewhere. The gypsum gateway was found complete, the lintel standing as it does at present.

To the left of the short passage that you enter now, a stairway runs up to the terrace above. The doorway into the Pillar Crypt beyond had originally a wooden lintel; this had perished and the blocks above had fallen inwards. To facilitate excavation it was therefore immediately replaced in cement. Note that the method of locking the door is the same as that employed in the South House (see page 66), while outside is a small hole to introduce a peg round which cord could be wound to seal the door from without.

The Pillar Crypt was found in an extraordinary state of preservation. The two pillars themselves were standing to their full height as was also the whole of the finely cut masonry of the lower story. Some concrete beams have had to be put in to strengthen the whole, but in the top course can easily be

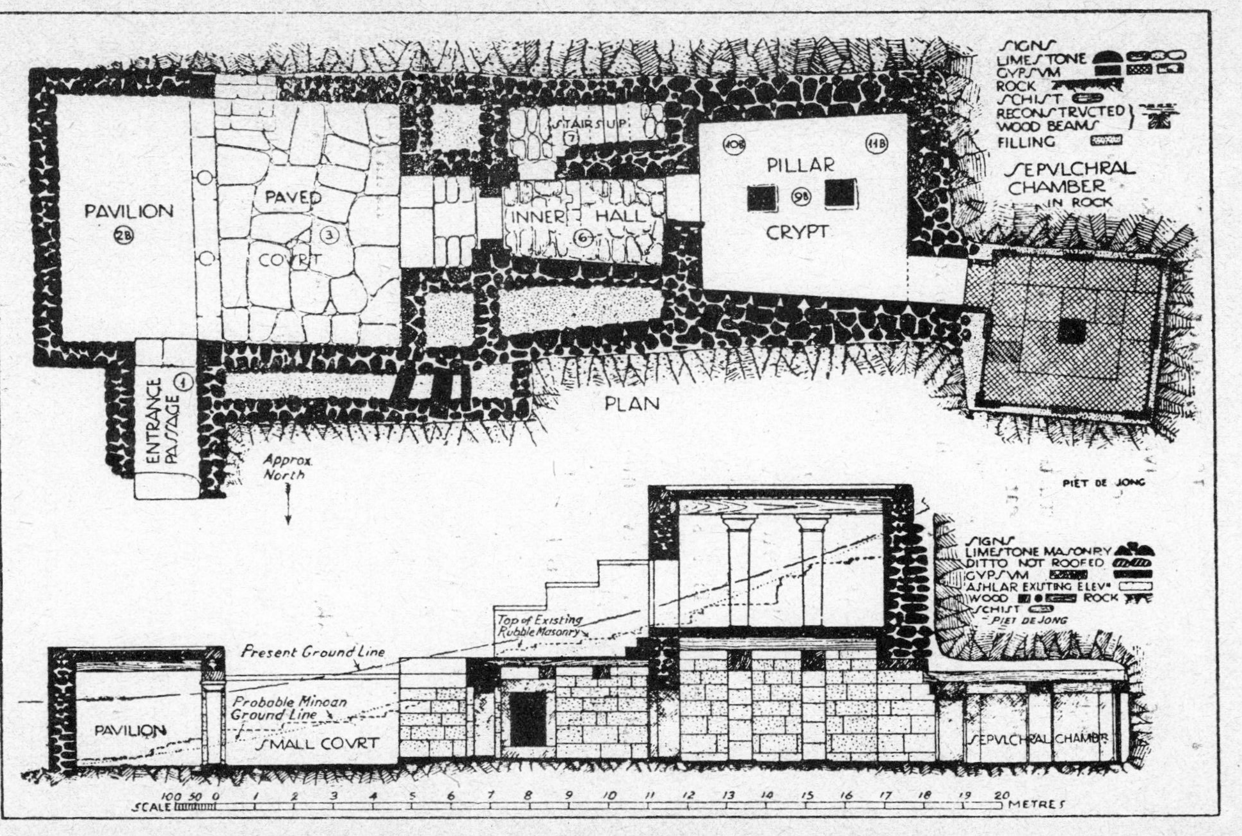

8 BASEMENT PLAN AND SECTION OF THE TEMPLE TOMB

made out the slots to receive the rafters. The sockets for beams and rafters gave the exact method of construction. Much of the rough masonry of the upper story is also in position (see below). Shortly after its construction in M.M. III much of the tomb was destroyed by an earthquake, and stones were taken from both the Pavilion antae and the pylons and used to wall up the spaces between the pillars. In the deep enclosures thus formed was found a mass of burials; but throughout, a passage was left open to the tomb-chamber proper.

This chamber opens off the north-west corner of the Pillar Crypt. It is about twelve feet square with a square gypsum pier in the middle surrounded by the usual depressions in the gypsum paving, and lined with upright slabs of gypsum about six feet high. These slabs were held back at the corners and in the middle of each side by key slabs. These in their turn were kept in position by two huge cross-beams which ran across the central pier. The roof was originally the rough rock. It was painted a deep Egyptian blue so that the dead man lying back would, as it were, see the heavens through a square window. When the tomb chamber was excavated the beams had perished and the roof had collapsed. The dampness of the soil had literally eaten away the base of the pillar and much of the lower parts of the side slabs. These, therefore, have been strengthened with cement, and a waterproof roof has been put on.

It is probable that the original coffin was of wood, with incrustations of precious metal, but at the very end of the Palace Period (L.M. II) a man, in whom we may perhaps see the last Minos of Knossos, was buried here. There is a small pit in the north-east corner and much of his funeral furniture was found. We may even have parts of his body, for in the doorway were the skull and some of the bones of a short athletic man of middle age.

The stairway, mentioned above, which runs up from the passage, leads to a terrace which runs not only over the passage but also over a space to the north. Here there is another entrance, from the north, at the higher level; and hence access was gained to the roof of the Pavilion, the way running over stone beams which span a narrow space north of the open Court.

From this terrace, also, was entered the upper story above the Pillar Crypt, much of the walls of which remain – rough stone originally plastered red. There were almost certainly two columns, corresponding to the two square piers below. The horns which stand here may have crowned the façade or have stood within. It is also possible that access to the Pillar Crypt below was obtainable by means of a trap-door, for – as the workmen said on seeing the method of locking the lower door – 'dead men do not lock themselves in'.

The whole tomb bears a striking resemblance to that described by Diodorus Siculus as having been built for Minos in Sicily – a tomb below and a temple of the goddess above.

GENERAL INDEX

(*Italic figures indicate illustrations*)